SELF-DIRECTED WRITERS

Leah Mermelstein

SELF-DIRECTED WRITERS

The Third Essential Element in the Writing Workshop

Foreword by **Matt Glover**

HEINEMANN
Portsmouth, NH

Heinemann

361 Hanover Street

Portsmouth, NH 03801–3912

www.heinemann.com

Offices and agents throughout the world

The author and publisher wish to thank those who have generously given permission to reprint borrowed material:

Excerpt from L. M. Guglielmino. 1978. *Development of The Self-Directed Learning Readiness Scale.* Ph.D. dissertation, University of Georgia, 1977. *Dissertation Abstracts International* 38 (11A): 6467A. University Microfilms No. AAC78-06004. Reprinted with permission. Available at www.lpasdlrs.com.

Credits continue on page xv.

Library of Congress Cataloging-in-Publication Data

Mermelstein, Leah.

    Self-directed writers : the third essential element in the writing workshop / Leah Mermelstein.

       pages cm

    Includes bibliographical references.

    ISBN 978-0-325-04800-0

    1. English language—Composition and exercises—Study and teaching (Elementary).

2. Language arts (Elementary).   3. Self-culture.   4. Independent study.   I. Title.

    LB1576.M456 2013

    372.6—dc23   2013017149

Editor: Holly Kim Price

Production: Patty Adams

Cover and interior designs: Suzanne Heiser

Typesetter: Gina Poirier Design

Manufacturing: Steve Bernier

Printed in the United States of America on acid-free paper

17 16 15 14 13 VP 1 2 3 4 5

Dedicated to my unborn child

who I know will bring

unimaginable amounts of joy

and happiness to my life

CONTENTS

FOREWORD

This book is important for many reasons, but for me the most important is that Leah decided to write it at all. Her decision to write this book came from a deep belief in the importance of guiding students to become self-directed decision makers. I frequently encounter educational environments where there is a disconnect between what adults say is important and what is actually happening in classrooms. Business and educational leaders call for college graduates to be innovative thinkers who are able to collaborate and solve problems creatively. But at the same time, more and more classrooms are falling into a one-size-fits-all model where all students receive the same teaching at the same time on the same day. Students are lost in a sea of standards and data. Leah attacks this disconnect by showing us how students can become self-directed, engaged decision makers while working in a context of standards.

It's this process that enables students to continually make decisions about what to work on in their writing and how to work on it.

Leah believes that teachers impact children's ability to be self-directed. Because she values the actions of teachers, she shares stories of teachers and of classrooms filled with self-directed learners—classrooms similar to Emily Callahan's fourth-grade class. Even though they have never met, Leah and Emily are kindred spirits because Emily's students embody the self-direction that Leah cares about so greatly. During a visit one morning, I saw Emily's students highly engaged in a variety of writing projects. Students were deep into a unit of study on how authors use engaging text structures. Students were able to choose not only their topics but also their genres as they learned to match audience, purpose, and genre. Here are just a few of the projects kids were working on:

- a sequel to an earlier story called "A Case of the Mondays"
- a story written as the diary of a person searching for Bigfoot

- a question-and-answer book about dolphins, developed from a survey of the student's classmates that asked them what they wanted to know about dolphins
- a heartfelt ABC text about a child's family
- a fantasy story with a repeated line structure

The rest of the class displayed a similarly wide range of topics and genres. As Leah says, "the benefit of this type of unit is that kids get to revisit previously taught genres, which deepens their understanding of them. Not only that, but they also discover which genres are their favorites and can spend more time writing and honing their skills in those genres" (5).

Writing like this doesn't happen by accident. I see similar lists of topics and genres whenever I'm in a classroom where students have high levels of authentic choice and self-reliance. It stems directly from the classroom environments and interactions between students and teachers throughout the year. Most importantly, it comes from teachers who, like Leah, value student self-direction.

Leah describes the process of children becoming self-directed like this: "It's this process that enables kids to become the bosses of their own learning. It's this process that teaches kids to use a wide variety of strategies to solve their own problems. It's this process that enables students to continually make decisions about what to work on in their writing and how to work on it. It's this process that keeps them engaged and producing high-quality work throughout the entire writing workshop" (8).

In these classrooms self-direction didn't occur at a special time of year or in a free-choice unit during the last two weeks of school. Nor was it something that occurred early in the year and was then forgotten. Instead this autonomous learning and writing was the result of a year-round effort made by the teachers. As Leah explains, "creating independent and self-directed writers is a yearlong project, not a September project" (10).

Leah shows you how self-direction is different from independence. Students, and adults, can work independently, but just being able to work on your own doesn't mean that you are productive. Not bothering the teacher might be a sign of independence, but it isn't necessarily a sign of working productively. Self-direction, on the other hand, means that students are taking action. They're setting a course for themselves. Self-direction is a much more valuable lifelong skill because it means two things. First, it means you have a direction. You are working toward a goal. You've charted a path and are working step-by-step to arrive where you want to be. Second, it means that you are making decisions. You aren't self-directed if someone else is deciding what you should do each day.

Just valuing self-direction isn't enough though. Students don't become self-directed because teachers get out of their way. Instead, they do so because their teachers take on an active, thoughtful role. Leah highlights specific classrooms and teachers that nurture self-direction. She gives you a glimpse into these classrooms, not only showing you what students are doing but also revealing the specific teaching moves that result in self-directed learners. These classrooms and teachers give us a vision for what's possible.

What makes this book truly special is that Leah takes the idea of self-direction a step further. She advocates for self-directed teachers as well. It's difficult to expect students to be self-directed if their teachers aren't. Leah shows the need for harmony between how students make decisions about their writing and how teachers make decisions about their teaching. Leah shows you how to make critical decisions that only a teacher who knows her individual students well can make. Programs, standards, and curriculum guides can't determine what an individual child needs on a specific day. Decisions about how to interact with a student are best made by a thoughtful, self-directed teacher.

In each chapter, Leah provides you with practical strategies for supporting self-directed writers during writing workshop. She describes environments and classroom routines that will help your students become self-reliant without you. She shows you how to plan curriculum and units of study that foster self-direction. And she illustrates how student-teacher interactions in focus lessons, conferences, and shares can reinforce self-direction each day.

In addition to practical strategies, Leah shares important concepts about teaching that apply to any content area. You'll learn about the importance of lingering longer. You'll be asked to consider the difference between "praise and being positive." You'll see the importance of "embracing uncertainty." Leah helps us envision writers who are confident, engaged risk takers who independently solve problems. They are excited, persistent, and resilient writers who are self-starters. They are resourceful writers who work toward important goals.

This book will spark a change in how teachers interact with their students each day. It will help parents think about how they want their children to think. And it will help educational leaders deeply consider what they value and how teachers can foster those same values. Classrooms that actively nurture self-directed writers should be *common* in schools, now more than ever.

Matt Glover

ACKNOWLEDGMENTS

I wrote this book on nurturing self-directed learners at a very fitting time in my life. Over the nine months it took me to complete the book, I learned firsthand about how important it is to be self-directed. I got the news that Heinemann accepted my book proposal on the same day that my pregnancy for my first child was confirmed. The goal was to finish the book by December 1st because I was due to give birth on December 31st. I knew that the next nine months of growing a book and a baby at the same time were going to be a busy but wonderful adventure. But I couldn't have imagined what else was in store for me.

People talk about how pregnancy should be a calm and serene time. This was not exactly the case for me. During those nine months while I was pregnant and writing this book, my father contracted a rare blood disorder. A few weeks later, I caught head lice and food poisoning during the same week. Shortly afterward, I attended my cousin's wedding, where the father of the groom (my uncle) passed out before dinner and was rushed to the hospital. And now I am writing these acknowledgments, pregnant, by flashlight on my iPad while stranded in my house because of Hurricane Sandy. Throughout all of that, I remained persistent in moving this book forward. I wrote this book during fifteen-minute breaks at work, in doctor's offices, at the hospital, as well as in between throwing up from food poisoning and pregnancy-induced nausea. I'm happy to finally slow down and take a moment to thank everyone who made this possible.

First, I would like to thank Matt Glover for writing the foreword to my book. Matt has always been one of my literacy heroes and I was lucky enough to work with him a few years ago. Our work together was seamless because our vision for what kids and teachers need is so similar.

Many teachers and literacy leaders contributed to the thinking in this book. I would like to thank Lorena Tesbir and Marnie Gleissner from King Street School in Danbury, Connecticut. They read many of the chapters in this book and gave me thoughtful critique on what else was needed to help teachers. Most importantly, they invited me into their classrooms and let me watch self-directed learners in action. A special thank-you goes to Gregory Scails and Tiny Hislop, the principal and assistant principal at King Street School. They set up schedules and freed up teachers to make the research in their school possible. Special thanks go to Christine Pruss and Pam Dalton, whom I have had the pleasure of working with in Danbury over the past few years. Both of them are amazing leaders in the district who always make sure that the staff development in their district is pertinent and pushes teachers to try new things. Christine was also the first person to question the phrase *independent writers*, saying that her vision for students during writing workshop was bigger than that.

I would also like to thank Trudy Cioff from Swanton Elementary School in Swanton, Vermont. Trudy piloted many of the ideas in this book and was always excited to revise her thinking as well as her teaching plans. I thank Robyn Brislin, Brent Coon, and Dena St. Amour for setting up and supporting the work in Trudy's classroom, as well as for leading the school and the district in powerful ways. Kosha Patel, Deb Baucher, and Patty McDermott were also instrumental in keeping the goal of self-directed learners at the forefront of the work in this district.

Sharon Fiden at PS 230 in Brooklyn, New York was a constant support for me throughout the writing of this book. Her answer is always yes when it comes to anything I ask. Both she and the teachers at PS 230 have contributed in many ways to the thinking in this book. Thanks to Freya Grice, the assistant principal at PS 230, for always setting up thoughtful work at the school. A special thank-you to Mary Murphy, the literacy coach at PS 230, as well as to all of the teachers for collecting writing and engaging in many conversations about the importance of self-directed learning during the writing workshop.

Special thanks also go to Bobbe Pennington and Paula Jensvold at Rick Marcotte Central School in South Burlington, Vermont for opening up their wonderful classrooms to me. Both of them read my book cover to cover and tried things in their classrooms as a result of it. I spent a fabulous morning watching their kids in action. It was thrilling to see how self-directed their students were. A special thank-you to Sue Luck, the principal of the school, who helped arrange for my visit.

I also want to thank all of the teachers in the Harrison School District in New York for thinking about this idea with me well before I wrote the book. A very special thank-you also goes to Marina Moran and Michael Greenfield for being amazing administrators who always push their teachers to think outside the box.

I also want to thank every teacher I have had the pleasure of working with during in-school visits as well as during presentations. Every question, every comment, and every story that teachers have shared with me have in some way contributed to this book. I thank the readers of my blog for commenting and pushing back on my thinking. I especially want to thank Jennifer Luff from Somers Point School District in New Jersey. In one of her blog comments, she suggested the term *self-directed* to describe what I was writing about.

Of course, I thank Lucy Calkins. Lucy mentored me early on in my career and helped me truly understand writing workshop. Lucy always stretches and revises her thinking and has taught me to do the same. I will forever be grateful for the support and guidance she provided me early on. I also want to thank the entire team at Heinemann for their hard work in putting this book together. Special thanks go to Holly Price. Holly has been an amazing editor and friend. All of her suggestions for the book were spot-on. I thank her for that and for understanding and being incredibly supportive of my timetable to get this book completed before my baby girl arrived. A special thanks also goes to Patty Adams, my production editor, who calmly took me through the production process.

My thanks for this book go beyond just the people who helped me with the writing of it; the people who kept my life together and supported me during this busy, wonderful (and sometimes stressful) time period were equally important. There are too many friends and family to thank each one personally, but I would like to take a moment to thank a few by name.

I want to thank Ellen Dillon and Shawn Brandon, my two closest friends. It's not surprising since I met them at the start of my teaching career. While teaching, we planned and taught and laughed together. Now, years later they kept me from losing it during this entire project. Whether they calmed my fears, made me laugh, or took me in during the hurricane, they were always there to alleviate the stress I was feeling and refocus me on what truly mattered. Both of them are going to be in the delivery room with me when I give birth and there is nothing that brings me more peace than that.

Erica Denman, my "mom mentor," talked me through not only teaching ideas but parenting ideas as well. She immersed me in all that I needed to do to prepare for my first child and did so with the greatest of patience and love. Thanks also to my cousins, Allison Faver and Michele Denman, who also were true mentor moms. Robin Epstein was instrumental in helping me design a home that is peaceful and serene and ready for the messy but wonderful work of a newborn.

I couldn't have made it through those intense months without the support of my family. My sister, Hayley, and my sister-in-law, Anne, carried all of my baby supplies up five huge flights of dark, rainy stairs when I had no elevator or power because of Hurricane Sandy. Both Anne and my brother, Josh, patiently installed my car seat, and my parents, Terry and Lothar Mermelstein, always knew just what to say and just what to do to keep my mind focused on writing and getting ready for my child.

And finally, I thank my unborn little girl, who I know will bring unimaginable amounts of joy and happiness to my life. Throughout the book, I talk about the importance of deadlines and celebrations as a way to stay self-directed. Imagining my life with her kept me on track and helped me stay focused, energized, and excited. Now that the book is complete, I can't wait to hand it in and experience the next exciting chapter of my life as her mother.

Leah Mermelstein
www.bestwritingconsultant.com

Credits continued from page iv

Photography Credits:

Cover: © Getty Images/Image Source/HIP
Chapter 1: © Image Source/Getty Images/HIP
Chapter 2: © JUPITERIMAGES/BananaStock/Alamy/HIP
Chapter 3: © Rubberball/Nicole Hill/The Agency Collection/Getty Images/HIP
Chapter 4: © Mel Yates/Digital Vision/Getty Images/HIP
Chapter 5: © Creatas/Jupiterimages/Getty Images/HIP
Chapter 6: © David Fischer/Digital Vision/Getty Images/HIP
Chapter 7: © Park Street Photography/Houghton Mifflin Harcourt/HIP
Chapter 8: © Houghton Mifflin Harcourt/HIP

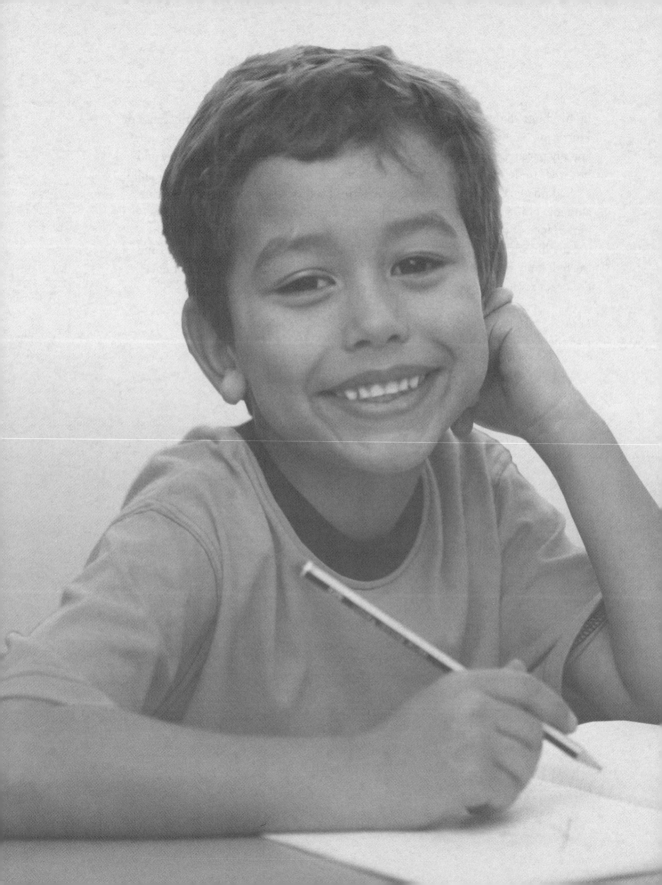

CHAPTER

THE ESSENTIAL ELEMENTS OF A WRITING WORKSHOP

It was early spring and I was visiting Donna Amato's first-grade classroom in the midst of her writing workshop. When I walked into Donna's classroom, she was busy conferring with her students, but regardless of that, the other kids were hard at work. They were excited, engaged, and producing high-quality, very individualized writing pieces. If and when they encountered problems, they seemed to seamlessly solve them by checking charts, asking friends, referring to texts, or simply taking a moment to process a possible solution. At the end of this amazing writing workshop, when Donna gathered her kids for the share session, she said, "We're about to gather for a share. You all have an important decision to make and I want you to make the decision that is best for you. Some of you might feel it's a better use of your time to keep writing. If that's true, don't come to the share today. Others might feel as though a conversation might spark an idea or help you solve a problem. If that's true, join us at the share meeting today."

The kids who didn't come to the share continued writing. Nobody (really and truly, not one single student) made a bad decision or fooled around while Donna conducted the share session with only some of her students. Rather, the students who didn't come were deeply engaged in their writing. Donna didn't have a special class or perfect kids. She was a special teacher who made deliberate teaching decisions that enabled her to run her classroom in this manner.

giving students options — not everything works for 1 student

The Writing Workshop

Before I dive into what made Donna Amato's writing workshop special, I want to first define what a writing workshop is and share its essential elements. I was fortunate enough to spend four years working at the Teachers College Reading and Writing Project at Columbia University with Lucy Calkins. It was there that I deepened my understanding of writing workshop.

In a writing workshop, kids usually choose their own topics. In the K–2 classroom, kids typically store their writing in writing folders. They use paper with space for both a picture and words so that the paper they use looks very much like the books they read. Some teachers staple these pages into books before kids begin writing, while others have kids take single pages and then staple them together when they've completed a book. Once kids get comfortable, many teachers have both options available in their classrooms. In a 3–5 classroom, kids typically begin the writing process in their writer's notebooks. A writer's notebook is a place to plan, think, and prepare for a draft. Once students are ready to draft, they typically leave their notebooks and store their drafts in folders on loose-leaf paper or in booklets (very much like the K–2 students). Many teachers ask what I think of having students store their drafts in their notebooks rather than in folders. While I understand it feels more manageable to have everything in one place, when teachers do this kids tend to use their notebooks to collect drafts rather than to think, plan, and prepare.

getting kids — comfortable

Writing workshop begins with a *focus lesson*, or *minilesson*, that lasts between five and fifteen minutes. This is a time when you gather the whole class and teach the students something that will lift the level of what they are doing. The topics of the focus lessons might span from elements of a particular genre, to a craft technique, to conventions, or even to how to navigate a part of the writing process. I personally prefer the term focus lesson to minilesson because it reminds you that the instruction during this time is short not because it's unimportant, but because it is focused on just one strategy or skill. Typically, subsequent focus lessons don't jump quickly to new material. Instead, a teacher will watch her students interact with the content taught and, if needed, will stick with that content over a series of days to deepen their understanding as well as to address possible confusion or misunderstanding. Often, a teacher will stick with a teaching point by using a picture book or some other type of text to teach the concept. A text used to help students understand a craft technique is called a *mentor text*. A teacher might also try the skill or strategy out in her own writing by modeling both her thinking and how that thinking led to her final product. She might also use a piece of student writing to reinforce the skill or strategy.

After the focus lesson, there is a work time that typically lasts anywhere from thirty to forty-five minutes (although it might be shorter at the start of the year). During this time, the teacher is busy conferring either one-on-one with kids or in small groups. Some wonderful resources for conferring with student writers are Carl Anderson's two books *How's It Going?* (2000) and *Assessing Writers* (2005) as well as his multimedia resource Strategic Writing Conferences (2009). The students who are not working with the teacher are writing independently. This independent portion of writing workshop is the focus of my book and typically one of the most challenging aspects of implementing a successful writing workshop because getting kids to work well independently is not always easy.

Finally, the writing workshop ends with a share, which is a time that should be both celebratory and instructional. My book *Don't Forget to Share* (2007) is a place to go if you want further information about this important element of writing workshop.

Element Number One: Daily Writing Time

A writing workshop is a daily period of writing instruction, which lasts for about forty-five minutes to an hour (although it might be shorter at the start of the year). If it's impossible for you to schedule a daily writing workshop, then at least try to schedule it three to four times a week. With less frequency than that, it's nearly impossible for kids to become engaged in the process because they are unable to count on a consistent time to work on their writing.

When teachers cannot schedule a daily writing workshop they often ask me if it's more beneficial to cluster the days together or scatter them throughout the week. Although there is no right or wrong answer to this, I personally would cluster the days together. When working on my own writing, it's always better if I have a few days in a row to write as I tend to get more engaged in the writing process. If I write on Monday and then don't write until Thursday or Friday, it takes me longer to get my mind back into my writing project.

Element Number Two: Long-Range and Ongoing Planning

Not only is it important to conduct a daily (or almost daily) writing workshop, but you also must plan for this time. One way you can do this is through long-range planning. Many teachers and districts plan for the long term by creating curriculum calendars (or curriculum maps). Curriculum calendars are essentially your plans for a year of writing instruction. They include the units of study that you plan on doing, the approximate amount of time each study will take, and the order in which you plan on doing them. Typically, a curriculum calendar includes a variety of different types of units. For example, some units are genre-based units. In a genre-based unit, kids continue to choose their own topics but write in a specific genre.

learning
— new genre hunting

This type of unit is fantastic for teaching kids a new genre or going deeper into a genre they have studied in a previous year. What is problematic about this type of unit is that although kids still have choice in topic, they lose their choice in genre.

To balance this out, there should also be some units that are more focused on either parts of the writing process or particular conventions or craft techniques. In these units, kids are able to choose both their topics and the genres that they will write in. For example, a teacher or district might include a rereading unit of study on a curriculum calendar. During this unit, the teacher would teach focus lessons that would assist students in becoming more adept at rereading their writing. Students would be asked to try out these rereading lessons but would be able to try them in topics and genres of their choice. The benefit of this type of unit is that kids get to revisit previously taught genres, which deepens their understanding of them. Not only that, but they also discover which genres are their favorites and can spend more time writing and honing their skills in those genres. For all of these reasons, I find a balance between different types of units on a curriculum calendar particularly helpful.

It's also helpful to plan ahead for what some of the teaching inside of the individual units on a curriculum calendar might be. Many teachers do this by thinking through what some of the intended unit goals might be. They also decide which texts to use within the unit, as well as what some of the focus lessons might be. Some great resources for helping you with both curriculum calendars and unit planning are *Units of Study for Primary Writing: A Yearlong Curriculum* (2003) and *Units of Study for Teaching Writing, Grades 3–5* (2006), by Lucy Calkins and colleagues from the Teachers College Reading and Writing Project, and *Projecting Possibilities for Writers: The How, What, and Why of Designing Units of Study*, by Matt Glover and Mary Alice Berry (2012).

Many districts and states have also adopted the Common Core State Standards (CCSS). These standards are yet another helpful resource when doing long-range planning. It's tempting, especially with the buzz surrounding them, to plan by first looking at the CCSS and then creating curriculum calendars and unit plans based upon them. I don't think that is a good idea. I believe it's essential to start first with conversations about what your hopes, dreams, and expectations are for the kids you're working with in the area of writing. After having those conversations, create a curriculum calendar that reflects those beliefs. Only then would I bring the Common Core State Standards into the picture. Specifically, I would hold the standards alongside the already completed curriculum calendars and unit plans and make revisions where the skills and strategies included in the standards are not reflected in your current plans.

look @ CCSS / make second / first plan

If you look at the Common Core State Standards as the final step rather than the first step, you are likely to create a plan that covers many of the CCSS without even realizing it. Doing this also enables you to have a deeper conversation about the CCSS because you are putting them into a context. Specifically, your prior teaching experiences, your conversations about your teaching, and your curriculum calendars will bring clarity to the standards and help you understand how the language in the Common Core document could play out in real-life classrooms! It's also important to keep in mind that the Common Core State Standards reflect the bare minimum of what you should accomplish in any one year. You want to exceed these standards. You have a much better chance of doing this if you start with your hopes, dreams, and expectations and then move to looking at how the CCSS connect to them.

Alongside this long-term planning, there should also be ongoing planning for your writing workshop. One of the districts I work with in Danbury, Connecticut helps teachers integrate both long-term and ongoing planning into their year. Teachers in this district do the long-term planning by beginning each school year with a curriculum calendar as well as a general outline for each of the units on their curriculum calendar. The district provides both of these to them. The district deliberately does not include a day-by-day sequence of what their focus lessons will be. It trusts that teachers will figure this out during their ongoing planning.

In their book *Projecting Possibilities for Writers*, Matt Glover and Mary Alice Berry (2012) make a good argument for why teachers shouldn't preplan a sequence of lessons, but rather should make those decisions as the Danbury teachers do, in the midst of teaching a unit. They say, "When you create a unit of study, it's tempting to think you know exactly what will happen on day five or day thirteen or eighteen of a unit of study. But, in reality you can't know what will happen on day thirteen until you and your students live the twelve days that come before it. In fact, the only way you can know what will happen on day thirteen is if you decide to ignore students for the first twelve days and teach by strictly adhering to a plan, blind to what is happening in your class each day" (2).

can't map out — day-to-day

The educators I work with in Danbury understand and agree with this idea and plan accordingly. They know that they'll figure out the exact sequence of lessons by watching and listening to their kids. They might discover that in the midst of their unit, their students need further instruction on particular lessons, or perhaps they'll see a need for lessons that they hadn't originally planned for. Because they haven't confined themselves to a predetermined sequence of lessons, they can respond to all of this. Long-term planning helps your teaching be more thoughtful and intentional, but your ongoing planning helps ensure that your day-by-day teaching is responsive to your students' strengths and needs.

Element Number Three: Self-Directed Learners

So far, I've outlined two essentials of writing workshop:

1. A daily or nearly daily period of writing workshop
2. Both long-range and ongoing planning

You may wonder, "Is this enough? Will all of my students be successful during writing workshop if I ensure that these two essential elements are in place?" These two essentials are not enough to produce the amazing results that Donna Amato achieved in my opening vignette. You may very well be conducting a daily writing workshop in your classroom now. You probably plan for this time on a regular basis, but if you are like the teachers that I work with, you might feel as though your writing workshop could be stronger. Perhaps some of your students finish early and ask the ever-popular question, "What should I do next?" Or some of your kids might periodically ask you for spelling help, a new writing idea, or a solution to a problem. The list goes on and on. It may be that some of your kids are able to work by themselves, but you wish that the quality of their work were stronger.

Donna's classroom stood out because during the independent phase of writing workshop, the kids were not coming to Donna for help. They were engaged, excited, and able to solve problems and continue doing high-quality work while Donna was busy working with other students. Achieving this self-reliance every day for every student was Donna's third essential of writing workshop. You might be tempted to use the word *independent* to describe Donna's kids because they certainly were working by themselves. In reality, her kids were doing something more rigorous than simply working on their own. Yes, they were independent, but they were also self-directed. This idea of being a self-directed writer is the focus of this book.

The third essential element of a writing workshop is the ability to create that dynamic process that you saw in Donna Amato's classroom. It's this process that enables kids to become the bosses of their own learning. It's this process that teaches kids to use a wide variety of strategies to solve their own problems. It's this process that enables students to continually make decisions about what to work on in their writing and how to work on it. It's this process that keeps them engaged and producing high-quality work throughout the entire writing workshop.

Accomplishing this goal for every kid in your classroom is exciting, but not easy. I can remember a time when I visited a first-grade classroom in Vermont. The teacher had asked me to do a revision lesson. Going into the lesson, I was worried that once the kids finished trying out what I was going to teach that day, they would either get off task or follow me around the room, asking me questions about what to do next. Sure enough, that is exactly what happened. Afterward, during our debriefing meeting, the teachers asked me for strategies on how to keep all of the kids engaged the entire time. At the time I didn't have the words to explain the solution, but I did know that the solution was much more involved than what we could possibly talk about in a half-hour debriefing period.

These days, it is still not uncommon for teachers to ask me to conduct a demonstration lesson that will get all of their kids working in this manner. I really do wish there were some magical lesson I could do to achieve this, but there isn't. Over the years, I've learned that creating self-directed writers takes a lot more than just one focus lesson or conversation. Donna and other teachers like her are able to accomplish this extraordinary feat because they view creating self-directed learners as essential to the success of their writing workshop, and this view drives every decision they make while planning and teaching.

● Misconceptions About Self-Directed Learning

Many teachers have the misconception that if you conduct a daily writing workshop where kids choose their own topics and you teach them strategies for being independent, then you are guaranteed independent and engaged writers. Although this certainly helps, unfortunately, it's not that easy. I've worked with teachers who had ongoing and beautifully organized writing workshops in their classroom. Children in their classrooms chose their own topics, and they taught their kids many routines and procedures. Even so, these teachers still had kids who either were not able to work well on their own or weren't growing as writers. Having a writing workshop is not enough to get kids to be independent and certainly not enough to get kids to look and sound like Donna Amato's kids.

Some teachers mistakenly believe that September is the only time to work on creating independent and self-directed writers. It's simply not true. As a matter of fact, that's how teachers run into trouble. They work with their students on this goal in September with the highest of hopes, and then October arrives and they are disappointed and frustrated because their students are unable to even work independently. Creating independent and self-directed writers is a yearlong project, not a September project.

Still another misconception is that our top students are the only ones capable of becoming self-directed learners. This couldn't be further from the truth! In Marnie Gleissner's first-grade classroom, she had done a lesson on how to use different tools around the room to help with spelling. A few minutes later, I watched Xavier, one of the more fragile students in the class, use his individual spelling list to find and then correctly spell the word *was*. What made this incident especially amazing was that Marnie hadn't spoken about that particular tool and Xavier had made the decision to do that on his own. My friend and colleague Lisa Burman once shared with me that in one of her most disadvantaged schools, the teachers have kids lead focus lessons (e.g., how to make a table of contents page or how to draw accurate diagrams). These are just two of many stories I know in which kids are incredibly self-directed. As you'll see throughout this book, all of our students can become more self-directed and it's important for us to pay attention to this skill with students at all levels. Very often, the ways that we teach our most fragile learners are counterproductive to creating self-directed learners. We must find ways to meet their needs as well as to help them become more self-directed.

How This Book Can Help

This book will help you create a classroom of kids who are able to work by themselves, who are excited and engaged, and who make decisions and solve problems on their own. This book will also help you become more self-directed. Hopefully, when you finish reading this book you'll be more comfortable working on your own without a curriculum plan that details every move that you'll make. Hopefully you'll feel more excited and engaged and more comfortable and equipped to make decisions and solve the inevitable problems that will arise in your classroom.

If you are new to writing workshop, you're going to want to read some of the texts that I suggested earlier in this chapter to get more information about the first two essential elements and then use this book at the same time as a resource for getting information about this third essential element. In that way, you'll be able to create a classroom filled with self-directed learners right from the start. If you are a more experienced writing workshop teacher, this book will be a great resource to help you refine your teaching to ensure that all of your students become more self-directed.

This book highlights six important components that need to be in place if you want to create a classroom of self-directed learners. Each of these components is addressed in its own chapter.

- You must create a physical environment that is easy for a child to navigate. The environment must allow kids to find multiple ways to get feedback on their writing other than the teacher. (See Chapter 3.)
- You must manage your classroom and create rituals and routines that keep the goal of self-directed learners at the forefront (see Chapter 4).
- You must scaffold your instruction so that all students can find their way into this instruction and be successful with it (see Chapter 5).
- You need to deliberately plan a yearlong curriculum with a focus on getting kids to become more self-directed (see Chapter 6).
- You need to deliberately plan units of study with a focus on getting kids to be more self-directed (see Chapter 7).
- You need to carefully craft focus lessons, conferences, small-group work, and share sessions so they not only teach kids new content but also guide them in becoming more self-directed (see Chapter 8).

There are three features you will find across many chapters in this book. The first feature will include assessment for self-directed learning which will help you evaluate students' autonomous learning. The second, "Collaboration in Action," will bring you into the classrooms I've been lucky enough to work in. You'll see how my collaborations with the teachers enabled us to tackle some difficult issues as well to discover ways to bring more self-directed learning into the classroom. The final feature, "Language Angled Toward Self-Directed Learners," will provide you with words that you can use in your teaching to promote more independent learning.

Sadly, Donna Amato, the exceptional teacher in my opening vignette, has passed away. The world has lost not only an amazing person but also an unbelievably intuitive, brilliant teacher. A colleague said to me that to keep her memory going, we need to, now more than ever, keep an eye toward helping teachers create classrooms like hers. This book is my tribute to Donna Amato. I wrote it with the hopes that it would help teachers around the world create classrooms of self-directed learners just like those in Donna's classroom!

> **"Creating self-directed learners improves the human race."**
>
> —ANGELA GALLAGHER, FIRST-GRADE TEACHER

CHAPTER 2

SELF-DIRECTED WRITERS:
The Third Essential Element of a K–5 Writing Workshop

Billy was busy at work in his kindergarten classroom. His teacher had done a focus lesson that day on how to use diagrams while writing an informational book. After the lesson, Billy included a diagram in his book. When he finished, there was time left and for a moment Billy was unsure about what to do next. I watched him as he walked up to one of the nonfiction charts in the classroom. After reading the chart for a few minutes, he gathered some paper and went back to his seat. He reread his book, added a page at the end of his book, and on that page began writing some page numbers next to the words. When I questioned him, he told me that he was making an index for his book. I then looked at the chart he had been reading; it was a brainstorm chart that included all the things the class had noticed earlier in the study about informational books. Sure enough, an index was one of the items on this chart.

Meanwhile, in the same classroom, Sara finished up her diagram at about the same time as Billy. Like Billy, she was unsure about what to do next. She sat for a while, twirled her pencil, played with her pencil box, and finally spent the rest of the time coloring her front cover blue. Both of these kids were independent. They worked by themselves. They stayed out of their teacher's hair. They kept themselves busy. But there was a difference. Both were independent; however, Billy was not only independent but also *self-directed*.

In Chapter 1, I emphasized that the missing essential element in many writing workshops is an emphasis on creating self-directed writers. While I was writing this book, many people questioned why I used the word *self-directed* and suggested that

I use the word *independent* instead. At the time I couldn't articulate the difference between those two terms but I knew that there was one. It's not that self-directed writers are not independent; they most definitely are. But you'll see in this chapter that independence is just one small aspect of being self-directed.

This chapter begins with some of the research surrounding self-directed learners. Then it expands upon what it means to be self-directed by discussing qualities that self-directed learners possess and then comparing self-directed learners with independent learners. Finally, it details the benefits you'll get in your classroom if you strive for self-directed learners.

Self-Directed Learning Is Important in All Stages of Life

In a paper titled *The Foundations for School Readiness* (Early Head Start National Resources Center at Zero to Three 1992, 3), the authors identified seven characteristics of children who are best prepared to thrive in school:

1. Confidence
2. Curiosity
3. Intentionality
4. Self-control
5. Relatedness
6. Capacity to communicate
7. Cooperativeness

Although these characteristics were not named as elements of self-directed learning but rather characteristics of school readiness, they certainly mirror many of the same characteristics I use when describing self-directed writers in the elementary classroom. While reading this list, I couldn't help but wonder how much more successful writing workshop would be if these characteristics were nurtured across the year in every unit of study, as well as in every focus lesson, conference, and share.

Not only has there been research about the importance of nurturing self-directed learners at the preschool age, but there has also been research conducted about self-directed learning and its impact on adults. Lucy M. Guglielmino (1978) developed the Self-Directed Learning Readiness Scale (SDLRS) initially for adults. Following are the eight factors she discovered to be essential for an adult learner to be self-sufficient:

1. Openness to learning opportunities
2. Self-concept as an effective learner

3. Initiative and independence in learning
4. Informed acceptance of responsibility for one's own learning
5. Love of learning
6. Creativity
7. Future orientation
8. Ability to use basic study skills and problem-solving skills

Once again, this list looks similar to the preschool list I shared earlier, as well as to the list of my hopes and dreams for self-directed students in the writing workshop. Both of these lists make me wonder what teachers can do and say during writing workshop to nurture these very characteristics at the elementary-school level.

Although Guglielmino's list was primarily created and used with adults, there is some research on how it relates to kids. After using this list with elementary students, researchers concluded that when children were not self-directed in elementary school, it often had to do with the "inefficiency of education systems in practice to let the capabilities of children to be actualized" (Nor and Saeednia 2009, 661).

It's not surprising to hear that schools have the power to either help or hinder kids in becoming more self-directed. This book will show you how to teach, plan, and speak in ways that nurture kids to become even more self-directed during writing workshop, as well as pave the way for them to become self-directed adults.

◼ Qualities That Describe Self-Directed Writers

In this book, I talk about nurturing elementary students into become more self-directed during writing workshop, but the truth of the matter is that these ideas go beyond writing and beyond elementary students. One of the things I learned while writing this book was the importance of paying attention to both the content taught during writing workshop and the qualities of self-directedness. For example, Paula Jensvold was teaching her first-grade students how to use mentor texts to create their covers for their final books. Not only was Paula teaching her kids one way to publish during writing workshop, but she was also nurturing resourcefulness as her kids were learning how to use mentor texts on their own. Throughout this book, you'll see examples of writing workshop teachers paying attention to both the content of writing as well as the qualities of self-directed writing.

Independent First and Interdependent Second

As I said earlier, an essential feature of being self-directed is the ability to work independently. I'd like to take this idea a step further and say self-directed writers make an effort independently before they enlist the help of others. I want to be clear that I'm not at all against students working together. I just don't want students to jump to asking for help too quickly when they in fact could do some or part of the work on their own. At the 2012 Literacy for All conference in Providence, Rhode Island, I heard Karen Caine speak about response groups in writing. One of the issues that she has seen in her work is that kids come to the response group and ask for feedback without doing any thinking on their own beforehand. She has found that response groups go better if the student who is sharing thinks before-hand about the kind of help he or she needs. This is a perfect example of independent thinking within a collaborative structure.

As quoted on the website ThinkExist, George Washington Carver once said, "I know of nothing more inspiring than that of making discoveries for one's self" (http://www.thinkexist.com). Self-directed writers constantly make discoveries on their own and are inspired by these discoveries. I often hear a common classroom mantra in my travels that has the potential to discourage self-discovery: "Ask three before me." In essence, this mantra is saying that when you have a question or a problem, you should ask three students before you approach the teacher. Although there are some benefits to this method, I find this saying problematic. Consider the following scenario: A third-grade student is writing and does not feel confident about his ability to spell conventionally. He is unsure whether or not he has spelled a certain word correctly. He wants to ask the teacher, but he remembers that he is supposed to ask three students before he approaches the teacher. He takes a moment and thinks about which kids in the class are the best spellers and he approaches one of them. That student is now interrupted from his writing and stops to help this child with his spelling. The first child gets the spelling help he needs without doing much work himself, and the second child is taken away from the important work he was doing. The "ask three before me" mantra potentially encourages kids to rely on others rather than rely first on themselves. As you can see in this example, the problem with that routine is that kids might be less likely to try things on their own if they know that the teacher encourages them to ask other kids. Figure 2.1 is a chart from Marnie Gleissner's first-grade classroom that nurtures the quality of being independent first and interdependent second. As you can see, the chart first features all of the things that kids can do on their own. The final strategy is to ask someone else.

Confident

Independence and confidence go hand in hand, because when you rely on yourself, you are bound to be more confident. For a moment, let's go back to the previous hypothetical example when one student asked another student for spelling help. The student now has the correct spelling—problem solved. Well, not really. The bigger problem still remains: the student who asked for help doesn't see himself as a good speller. More than likely, he will feel less confident about spelling after this experience rather than more confident. On the other hand, if he had been encouraged to try spelling the word himself first, he may have very well surprised himself with what he was able to do, thus building his confidence.

A concrete way to build confidence in students is to watch them work by themselves and then point out what they're doing on their own. I was working with Jayson, a second grader, who was doing very little on his own. On this particular day, he spent the first five minutes gathering his materials and then finally did spend a few minutes writing on his own. When I conferred with him, instead of focusing on the wasted time, I helped him realize what he did on his own. I said, "Did anybody help you get those words on the page, or did you do that by yourself?" With a big smile, he told me that he in fact had done that on his own. When I asked him how that made him feel, he said better. I loved his word choice of *better*. To me it seemed to be code for him feeling more confident in himself.

I often use share sessions at the end of writing workshop to build children's confidence by illuminating what they did on their own. In my book *Don't Forget to Share* (2007), I tell the story of a boy named Cameron who was causing all kinds of ruckus in the classroom and generally getting very little accomplished during

[handwritten margin note: boost confidence by telling them what they've achieved]

FIGURE 2.1 A CHART FROM MARNIE GLEISSNER'S FIRST-GRADE CLASSROOM ON STRATEGIES FOR WRITING TRICKY WORDS

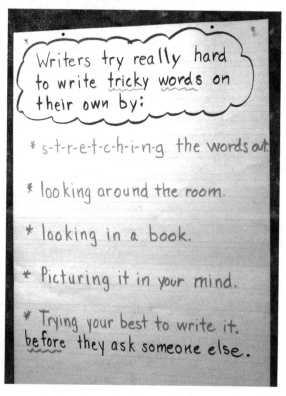

writing workshop. What turned him around was the day we gave him a "private office" that would allow him to write free of distractions. He wrote more that day than any other day in his life and we highlighted this accomplishment during that day's share session. His smile was huge and you could see his confidence growing in the midst of the share. His change in confidence level turned him around as a student. In *What a Writer Needs*, Ralph Fletcher says that a true mentor sees the potential in a student before the student sees it in himself (1993, 15). If we want our kids to become more confident, we need to see their potential before they do.

Willing to Take Risks

During planning meetings, teachers often ask me if they should be concerned about particular students. One of the first questions I ask in response is whether or not the students are risk takers. The reason I ask is because I know that when a child is a risk taker, she is more likely to grow quickly. The student will be curious and try things that aren't always easy or comfortable. Being a risk taker goes hand in hand with being confident because when you're confident, you tend to take risks. Andre Malraux said, "Often the difference between a successful person and a failure isn't one who has better abilities or ideas but the courage that one has to bet on one's ideas, take a calculated risk—and to act" (quoted on ThinkExist, http://www.thinkexist.com).

I used to think that people were either risk takers or not risk takers depending upon their personalities. Now I believe that although personality does play a role, our teaching can transform non–risk takers into risk takers. Getting kids to be risk takers is dependent upon your own belief systems, language, and actions. For example, many teachers will talk to kids about doing the best they can while trying to spell a word. At times I see those very same teachers walking around the room, complimenting kids on spelling words correctly, unintentionally sending the message that correctness is more important than taking a risk. There is absolutely nothing wrong with letting kids know that you value spelling and the ability to spell words correctly. However, when nurturing the quality of risk taking, you'll want to highlight the kids who use challenging words in their writing and try to spell those words the best that they can, rather than compliment only kids who simply spell words correctly.

Engaged

In my travels, I've heard many teachers lament that their kids will do only the bare minimum during writing workshop. That is, they do exactly what the teacher taught during the focus lesson and no more. Self-directed writers behave differently. They are not writing only to please the teacher and to finish the assignment. They are engaged. The work that they are doing has caught their attention, their minds, and their energy. Because the work is bigger than the teacher or the assignment, they can typically work for longer periods of time. There are many ways that teachers can try to nurture such engagement. One way is to keep their feedback at the forefront of their teaching. When I was in Bobbe Pennington's fourth-grade classroom, she completed a lesson on how you can get ideas for personal narratives by starting with a feeling and then coming up with stories from your life that relate to that feeling. During her focus lesson, her conferences, and her share, she kept asking her students for their feedback and ideas. Her kids were incredibly engaged because it was clear that their input was welcomed and expected. They worked differently because they knew their teacher would be asking them for their thoughts.

Sometimes getting kids engaged is as simple as giving them title pages for their books or an engaged audience for their writing, but it can also be more complex, such as rethinking how to organize a unit of study. While looking at the Common Core State Standards, a first-grade teacher expressed concern that her kids would not be engaged if she asked them to do opinion writing (one of the text types in the CCSS document). Her concern led us to a very interesting conversation about the power teachers have to create curriculum that captures students' attention. We all agreed that if we gave each kid a piece of paper and asked the students to write down their opinions, they would more than likely be disengaged and do only the bare minimum. On the other hand, we felt that kids would be very interested if we began this unit of study by asking them what they felt was unfair in their lives and then showed them how they could take those opinions and write persuasive letters to people who might listen. That one conversation turned a potentially boring unit of study into a very engrossing one. Keep in mind that being engaged in your work does not necessarily mean that every day of writing is fun. Writing is hard work and some days are wonderful because you figure things out and some days are harder as you struggle to get your ideas on the page in clear and honest ways. Self-directed learners work through struggle, because they understand it is part of the writing process. Regardless of whether the work is easy or hard, fun or not so fun, if you're engaged, it occupies your time, energy, and mind.

Excited

I read a quote from William Butler Yeats on the blog *Jurasstastic* that sums up the excitement that self-directed writers have: "Education is not the filling of a pail, but the lighting of a fire" (http://www.jurasstastic.wordpress.com). Excitement is closely related to engagement, because when you are engaged in the work, it feels exciting, even on hard days. Self-directed writers view their work as a project, an adventure of sorts rather than just an assignment. They are drafting letters to their teacher because they want more lunch time. They are putting up signs in the bathroom to remind people to flush the toilet. They are writing stories about their lives to entertain their classmates. They are writing letters to their grandmas because they miss them. You can't teach excitement by saying, "Hey kids, be excited about your writing." Getting kids excited is not a focus lesson. It comes from the way you organize your classroom. It comes from the way you manage your room. It comes from the way you plan your units and what you say in your focus lessons, conferences, and shares. Every curricular decision I make is guided by what language I can use that will build excitement. I know if kids are excited, all else will fall into place.

Persistent

The word *persistent* is defined on *Oxford Dictionaries Online* as "continuing firmly or obstinately in a course of action in spite of difficulty or opposition." Albert Einstein once said, "It's not that I am so smart. It's just that I stay with problems longer." Albert Einstein was persistent. A self-directed learner expects difficulty to occur and is not surprised by it. It doesn't shatter her confidence and she does not take it as an indicator that something is wrong. She understands that difficulty is a natural part of the process and therefore doesn't give up when it occurs. Rather, she works harder knowing that her hard work will change the situation. You might be wondering how to get your students to become more persistent. I saw Marnie Gleissner conduct a lesson where she was nurturing persistence. Her lesson was on how to use classroom tools to get spelling help. While modeling, she tried out a few different strategies before she got the spelling she needed. Watching Marnie, I couldn't help but notice that not only was she teaching kids how to use tools in the room to get spelling help, but she was also modeling how to be persistent in solving a problem. She modeled trying a few strategies before she found one that worked for her. In this book, you'll discover lots of ways to nurture persistence, but it's important to realize that in order for kids to become more persistent, you must run your classroom with the belief system that hard work, not innate talent, is what will help your kids improve their writing. In *Opening Minds*, Peter Johnston talks about the differences between organizing your classroom with a dynamic learning frame and organizing your classroom with a fixed-performance learning frame. He says that in a dynamic learning frame, "problems/challenges/errors are to be expected if a person is taking on challenge—which is valued (even experts/authors make mistakes)" but that in a fixed performance frame, "problems/challenges/errors are indicators of one's intellectual ability" (2012, 17). If you want children to be persistent, you'll need to run your classroom within a dynamic learning frame.

Resilient

Resilience comes along with persistence. Whereas persistent is how you act in difficult situations, resilient is how you feel in difficult situations. *Resilience* is defined on *Merriam-Webster Online* as "an ability to recover from or adjust easily to misfortune or change." Peter Johnston states that "children who adopt a fixed performance frame tend to become helpless when they run into trouble. They cease being strategic except when it comes to ego defense" (2012, 15). Let's take, for example, a child who has finished her draft and is very excited. She shares it with some classmates and they ask some legitimate questions that reveal some flaws. Of course, there is bound to be some disappointment because the student has worked hard and originally thought the draft was almost finished, if not completely finished. Some students (or adults) in this situation get so sad, upset, or angry by this change of events that they are paralyzed and unable to cope. They shut down and say or think things such as, "I like it the way it is. My classmates are wrong," or "I stink as a writer." They don't handle change well and are unable to move beyond these feelings. Others are more resilient. Certainly, they will have some of these same feelings originally, but they recover quickly, adjust to the change of events, and look at their drafts with new eyes and develop a plan of action to improve them.

Across this book, you'll discover ways to help all of your students become more resilient by utilizing the dynamic learning frame that Peter Johnston talks about. Here's an example from Lorena Tesbir's classroom: Lorena was doing a lesson to help students find writing ideas. Throughout the lesson, she was very careful in her word choice, saying things such as, "All writers have days when they don't know what to write about." When a student piped up and said that the lesson didn't pertain to her because she already had a writing idea, Lorena said, "Well today is your lucky day. I'm sure there'll be days this year when you don't have an idea." She was deliberate in her word choice, she told me later, because she wanted kids to realize that even if they didn't have that problem that day, they might have that problem in the future. Yes, Lorena was teaching students how to find a topic idea, but she was also nurturing resilience; she was preparing students to expect and accept difficulties in the future.

Resourceful

Some students know how to get support for their writing only by asking the teacher or a friend for help. Resourceful writers use many types of support systems while working. Of course, if we want kids to be resourceful, then we must provide many types of support within the classroom. Billy, the kindergarten student I referred to in the opening of this chapter, was unsure about what to do next after he finished what the teacher taught during the focus lesson. He didn't say, "I'm done," nor did he ask a friend what he should do next. Instead, he deliberately went to a particular resource in the classroom, a chart that he thought could help, and got the idea to put an index in his book. You might be thinking that some kids in your class will do this automatically and some kids won't, as you saw in the earlier example with Sara. This book will show you how to help all students become more resourceful while writing.

Self-Starting

I once spoke with a fourth-grade boy who had been working on a chapter book during writing workshop for the past few years. He was still writing and publishing in all of the genres the class was studying, but he worked on this book whenever he had extra time during writing workshop. Another girl in second-grade was doing the same thing. Billy, in the opening example of this chapter, put an index in his book after seeing an index in other nonfiction books. In all of these cases, the teachers supported and encouraged kids to do these things but never mandated it. All of these students were self-starters. They went above and beyond what was taught in the focus lesson, conferences, and shares and invented new things they could do without teacher intervention. This is something only a few kids do. One of the goals of this book is to show you how to help all kids at all experience levels become self-starters.

Lorena Tesbir showed her kids a planning sheet they could use before writing a personal narrative. After making it, she realized that it worked well for some students but not as well for others. We decided that we could make planning more effective if kids designed their own planning sheets and then tested these sheets out to see if the plans they made improved their drafts. After thinking further, we realized that by doing this we were also nurturing kids to become self-starters. We pulled a small group of kids together—some who were strong writers and some who were more fragile—and we asked them to create some planning templates and then let us know if and how these planning templates improved their drafts. In Figures 2.2 and 2.3 you'll see two very different planning sheets created by

FIGURE 2.2 CHIARA'S PLANNING SHEET

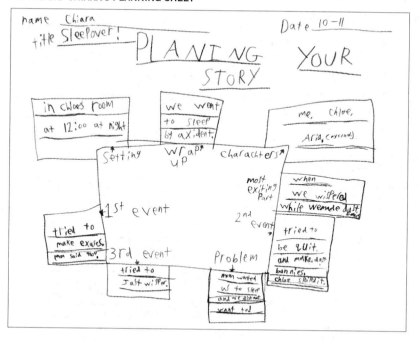

name Chiara
title Sleepover!

Date 10-11

PLANING YOUR STORY

in chloes room
at 12:00 at night

we went
to sleep
by axident.

me, chloe,
Aria, (myself).

Setting   Wrap up   charachters

1st event

tried to
make exuses.
mom said no.

3rd event

tried to
Just wisper.

most exiting part

2nd event

Problem

mom wanted
us to sleep
and we did not
want to!

when
we wispered
while we made dust bunnies.

tried to
be quit.
and make dust
bunnies.
chloe spoiled it.

Personal Narrative

Name Chiara

Date 10-12

SLeePover!!

On Saturday night, My freind Aria
came over to my house. We set up
our sleeping bags in chloe, my little
sister's room. Chloe got three chairs and
we made dust bunnies. it was eleven
o'clock in the night. mom and dad
were in bed. mom twould us to go
to sleep. Aria, me, and chloe came
up with the same face. It looked like
an "oh-oh" face! we trid lots of exusoe,
they did not work. next we tried to
make dust bunnies quietly. Chloe spoiled it
by talking alot and loud, then we tried to
just wisper. that did not work when Aria Started

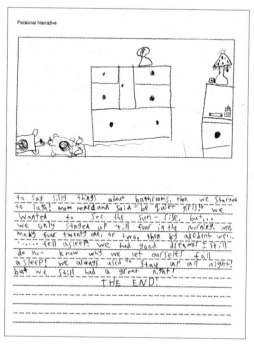

Personal Narrative

to say silly things about bathrooms, then we started
to lagh! mom heard and said "be quiet girls" we
wanted to see the sun-rise, but...
we only stayed up 'till four in the morning, well
maby four twenty one, or two. then by axedent we...
..... fell asleep. we had good dreams! Is it? I
do not know why we let ourselfs fall
asleep! we always used to stay up all night!
but we still had a great night!

THE END.

FIGURE 2.3 DYLAN'S PLANNING SHEET AND DRAFTS

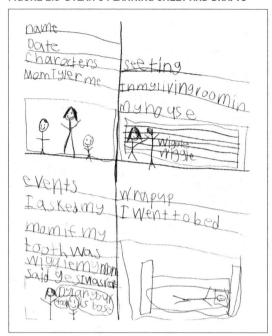

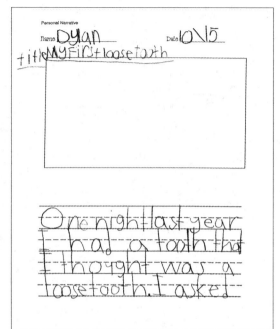

two very different kids. Both Chiara and Dylan used their planning sheets but in different ways. Chiara's planning sheet clearly helped her organize and put all of the parts of her story into her draft. Dylan's planning sheet helped him realize that what he really wanted to write about was not losing a tooth but the excitement he felt once he lost it. Even though his planning sheet is different from his draft, this thinking beforehand led him to find his focus.

Self-Regulating

Zimmerman (2000) identifies how a student's use of specific learning processes, level of self-awareness, and motivational beliefs combine to produce self-regulated learners. Self-regulated learners are self-aware, just as Zimmerman suggests, and are able to create reasonable and meaningful goals for themselves and determine whether or not they are meeting these goals.

Let's look at some work from Trudy Cioff's third-grade classroom, where she was deliberately trying to nurture these qualities. Trudy knew that if she simply

FIGURE 2.3 DYLAN'S PLANNING SHEET AND DRAFTS, *CONT.*

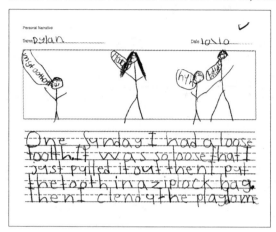

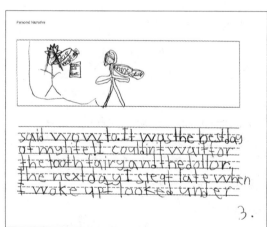

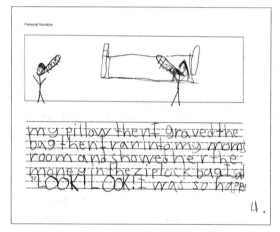

asked kids to make goals, they would be overwhelmed and perhaps create goals that either were not reasonable or were not needed. Instead she created a goal-setting sheet that narrowed kids' choices down, and she had them reflect upon whether or not they reached those goals. In Figure 2.4, you can see how Mattison used a goal-setting sheet to set reasonable goals and then reflect upon them.

Self-directed learners possess many more qualities than just the ability to work independently. In Figure 2.5, I compare the characteristics of self-directed learners and independent learners.

FIGURE 2.4 MATTISON'S GOAL-SETTING SHEET

Name: _Mattison.L_

Author's Goal Setting Sheet

Date	Today's goal...	What did I do today?
10\8	• Plan in my notebook ○ Draft ○ Re-read my writing ○ Add to or change my writing (revise) ○ Fix my writing (edit) ○ Other _____	Today I _planed in my note book and fineshed my book that I started today_
10/9 October	○ Plan in my notebook • Draft ○ Re-read my writing ○ Add to or change my writing (revise) ○ Fix my writing (edit) ○ Other _____	Today I _Starded a book and finesht it and Starded a book_
	○ Plan in my notebook ○ Draft ○ Re-read my writing ○ Add to or change my writing (revise) ○ Fix my writing (edit) ○ Other _____	Today I _____

FIGURE 2.5 QUALITIES OF SELF-DIRECTED LEARNERS VS. THOSE OF INDEPENDENT LEARNERS

Self-Directed Learners	Independent Learners
Independent first, interdependent second Confident Willing to take risks Engaged Excited Persistent Resilient Resourceful Self-starting Self-regulating	Keep busy Stay out of the teacher's hair Behave well Follow directions

● Benefits of Creating Self-Directed Learners

Self-directed learners are independent first and interdependent second. They are confident, excited, engaged, persistent, resilient, resourceful, self-starting, and self-regulating. So what are some of the ways both you and your students will benefit if you view self-directed learning as the third essential element of writing workshop?

Kids Will Get More Practice with What You Are Teaching

Think of how many more hours of practice kids would get if every day during writing workshop, they were working on what you had taught in your focus lessons, conferences, and share sessions across the year. With the Common Core State Standards asking for mastery, this practice time is crucial, and kids must understand how to use independent writing time to both practice what you've taught as well as explore new things on their own. If kids are self-directed, they will do just that. If they are not, much of this independent time will be wasted because they'll simply wait to work with you or do the bare minimum. Not only that, but when you see them trying things during the independent portion of writing workshop (especially when you haven't asked them to), you'll know that they are becoming more confident.

In addition, when kids practice, they reach a deeper level of understanding. Take, for instance, the use of dialogue in your writing. You use dialogue once and you understand that writers make people speak in their stories. If you practice it over and over again during writing workshop, you deepen your understanding and begin to recognize the finer details, such as how dialogue can help you better understand a character or the relationship between characters, how it can help you move the plot along, or the different types of words you can use when writing dialogue.

Kids Will Make Unique Decisions

During a keynote speech, Ian Dukes said that on average kids make a decision only every thirty-four minutes in school. That's not nearly often enough! How frustrating and limiting it must be to have such little control over your learning, and how freeing and empowering it must be to have more control and make more decisions. Kids who are self-directed tend to be more comfortable making decisions such as which charts to use, which goals to make for themselves, and what to do when they think they are finished. Teachers who aim for classrooms filled with self-directed learners often put kids in the position of making decisions, which in turn makes them more autonomous.

Even the most well-intentioned teachers don't always set up their classrooms to support and encourage kids to do this, which negatively impacts how kids use their independent time. During a visit to King Street Primary School in Danbury, Connecticut, I observed the students working on editing and revising their small moments. The teacher, Lorena Tesbir, had given the kids an editing checklist and they were using the checklist to edit their pieces. After the lesson, Lorena shared that she was not satisfied because although the checklist was helpful, it was also limiting. Some kids, for example, had checked their pieces but discovered that everything on the checklist was already correct. Those kids muddled through the rest of the writing workshop because they simply didn't know what else to do. Other students didn't understand how to do everything on the checklist and when they got to a hard part, they shut down or interrupted their teacher in the midst of a conference. Lorena wondered if she could revise her teaching so that kids understood how to use the checklist in ways that would suit their unique needs. Lorena's question and concern changed the course of her teaching. While teaching, she was much more aware of not only the content of what she was teaching, but also how to get kids of all levels to be more self-directed with that content.

Kids Will Go Beyond the Day's Topic

During our focus lessons or conferences, we usually teach kids a particular quality of writing that we hope they will try (that day or over the next few days). Teachers often say that kids are fine at the start of writing workshop, but once they try what the teachers have taught, they don't know what to do next. Some kids are obvious about the fact that they are done and will yell out, "I'm finished!" or follow you around the room. Others hide it better. They might sit quietly, doodle, and color in their pictures as a way to keep busy when they have finished the work of the day. In a classroom that is filled with self-directed learners, this doesn't happen. Kids have a wide variety of other things they can do that go beyond what was taught today.

You Will Be Able to Individualize Instruction

Often, teachers tell me that they find conferring and small-group instruction difficult because they are interrupted by students who are running into problems during writing workshop and don't know how to solve them. Self-directed writers understand that it is their job to solve problems, not their teacher's. Fewer interruptions mean teachers are better able to individualize instruction through conferences and small-group work.

● You Can Do This!

Independent, confident risk takers who are engaged, excited, persistent, resilient, and resourceful, as well as self-starters who self-regulate! Sounds wonderful, doesn't it? While writing and researching for this book, I discovered that achieving this goal with kids is hard work but definitely doable. Throughout the book, you'll not only see examples of kids who are working toward becoming more self-directed, but you'll see examples of teachers doing this as well. You'll see teachers who are independent, confident, engaged, excited, persistent, resilient, resourceful self-starters who also self-regulate, teachers who are able to bring this third and often missing element of writing workshop alive in their classrooms.

> "Education is knowing where to go to find out what you need to know; and it's knowing how to use the information you get."
>
> — WILLIAM FEATHER, AUTHOR AND PUBLISHER

CHAPTER 3

CREATING PHYSICAL ENVIRONMENTS THAT KIDS CAN EASILY NAVIGATE

It was early September and I was at South Street School in Danbury, Connecticut with a group of teachers. Our goal for that day was to study and discuss the classroom environments. Truthfully, I was not particularly excited. Although I am organized by nature, making things look pretty is not my forte. When I was a classroom teacher, I was always overwhelmed and intimidated by my colleagues' perfectly polished and beautifully decorated rooms, and now as a literacy consultant, I felt unsure about what to say to the teachers about classroom environments. I knew there was more to it than just aesthetics, but I didn't have the words to explain the bigger purposes, nor did I understand completely the power that classroom environments could have on student learning.

After spending just a few minutes in their classrooms, I began to understand. These teachers' charts, their mentor texts, and their supplies were sometimes beautiful but sometimes a bit more clumsy (like mine were as a teacher). What stood out in all of the classrooms, however, was that the kids used the resources not only to keep themselves engaged during the independent portion of writing workshop but also to solve the inevitable problems that arose. This day spent studying classroom environments was one of my most productive of the year, because it got me to think about the role that classroom environments play in creating self-directed learners.

In Chapter 2, I introduced the different qualities that self-directed writers possess. In this chapter you'll learn how the setup of your classroom can help kids become more resourceful, more independent, more persistent, more resilient, and better able to self-regulate their learning. I begin by sharing some of the common resources you'll want to make available in your classroom. Next, I share some of the roadblocks you might face with these resources and some possible solutions. Finally, I share some classroom environment tips to keep in mind throughout the year.

● Vital Classroom Resources

In order to have a successful classroom environment, you must give kids access to effective resources. In this chapter, I talk about four key resources:

1. Process and genre charts
2. Mentor texts
3. Writing centers
4. Student writing

You might be looking at this list and nodding, thinking, "Yes, of course. These resources are already an integral part of my classroom environment." Many teachers already have these tools in their classrooms, but having them does not guarantee that kids will use them in productive ways. I have seen far too many well-intentioned teachers fill their classrooms with beautiful examples of these resources, yet they still have kids who don't use them or use them unsuccessfully. How do you structure and organize these resources so that kids are able to successfully use them to solve problems and make important decisions?

Charts Develop Resourcefulness, Independence, Persistence, Resiliency, and Self-Regulation

Two main categories of classroom charts can provide support for your kids during writing workshop: process and craft charts. Process charts help students figure out ways to navigate parts of the writing process. For example, a chart titled "What Can You Do When You Think You Are Finished?" is a process chart because it will hopefully help kids keep themselves engaged in the writing process even after they feel they are finished. A craft chart, on the other hand, shows students specific ways to craft a part of a writing piece. Craft charts are more focused on qualities of writing. For example, a chart titled "Ways to End Your Persuasive Letter" is a craft chart. This chart would give kids a few options of how they could conclude their persuasive letters. The hope is that each kid would use this chart to play around with the ending of his or her own persuasive letter and ultimately figure out the ending that best matched that piece of writing without enlisting the help of the teacher or another student.

Simply having these process and craft charts available in your classroom is not enough. The next question is: How do you ensure that these charts are not just pretty decorations that your colleagues admire, but key resources for your kids? There are a few things you'll want to consider. First, you'll want to make sure that your chart gives kids some options but not too many. In my first few years of teaching I had a wonderful staff developer named Peter Sinclair. Once, when Peter was watching me create a chart with my kids, I had a moment of panic. I was nervous because the chart I was making had only a short list of options on it. Meanwhile, all of my colleagues had long, beautiful charts with many more options. Although their charts looked pretty, I found that my kids didn't use charts with lots of options. I thought that a chart with fewer options might be a more supportive resource for them. I was thrilled later when Peter complimented me on this decision. We spoke at great length about the importance of charts that kids would use versus charts that just looked pretty.

At times, too many options can be problematic. Imagine a chart with twenty options on it. Some kids will simply not use it because it can be overwhelming. Others might spend a good portion of their writing time unsuccessfully trying to use it. Ultimately, what you want are charts that kids can use seamlessly and quickly so that they can jump right back into their writing. The consequences of having too many options on a chart are more severe than kids simply being overwhelmed or not using the chart that day. In this situation, some are left feeling defeated and less likely to trust that the charts around the room will help them in the future. The feeling of being defeated leads to kids who aren't resilient, resourceful, or independent. In Chapter 2 I featured a chart from Marnie Gleissner's classroom titled "Writers Try Really Hard to Write Tricky Words By . . . ." On this chart, Marnie gave the kids five options, all of which she had modeled. In this example, there were certainly some options, but not too many.

There are times when lots of options do work for kids. You'll see in Chapter 7 I recommend that during the immersion phase of a unit of study you create a brainstorm chart that has many options for kids. What makes so many options work in this instance is that the chart is created over a week and the kids are the ones who put all of the options on the chart. Ultimately, you'll know if kids need limited options or more options by watching their ability to independently use the charts in your classroom.

You'll also want to clearly name the craft techniques on your craft charts as yet another support system for your kids. Lorena Tesbir created a chart titled "How Can We Begin Our Informational Books?" Not only did she have three options for how to start informational books, but she also clearly named each of these options. For example, one of the beginnings was named a "false information beginning." The moment that Lorena named the beginnings on the chart it moved the craft technique from something one adult author used to something that authors of all ages can use. She also included a speech bubble that said, "Hmm, could I try that in my writing?" This speech bubble was yet another support system that encouraged kids to use the chart.

You'll also want to consider the use of pictures for kids of all ages. It's important to use pictures that aren't just decoration or visual interpretations of the words but rather reminders of previous learning experiences. For example, Figure 3.1 shows a chart titled "Good Writers Do Many Things." Next to each option is a picture that reminded kids of a previous learning experience. By putting a relevant picture next to the words, the teacher gave all students access to the chart.

FIGURE 3.1 ALL KIDS HAVE ACCESS TO THIS CHART BECAUSE THERE ARE BOTH PICTURES AND WORDS.

Finally, you'll want to clearly explain the purpose of each chart to your kids. If they understand the purpose, they'll be more likely to use the chart. For example, while making a chart titled "What Should You Do When You Think You're Done?" you might say something like: "Children, there will be lots of times across the year when you'll feel like you're finished writing but there will be more time left. It's important that you use your time well and figure out what you can do without having to ask me or even a friend. Here is a chart that I started that will give you some ideas. You'll decide how you use that time, but let's take a look at this chart together so we can talk about it and add more to it if we think we should."

Explaining the purpose of a tool helps kids become more resourceful. It also helps them self-regulate their learning. Neither the chart nor the explanation tells kids exactly what to do. They'll need to use the resource to set their own goals and agendas for what to do. For more information on how to use charts effectively in the classroom, I highly recommend Marjorie Martinelli and Kristine Mraz's wonderful book *Smarter Charts, K–2: Optimizing an Instructional Staple to Create Independent Readers and Writers* (2012).

Mentor Texts Also Help Kids to Be Resourceful

There are many different types of mentor texts as well as many purposes for using them. Here I talk about mentor texts that will support your kids in the area of writing. Many teachers use mentor texts in their focus lessons or conferences, but fewer have them available as resources for kids to use independently. Other teachers do put them out, but kids don't use them very well. Both of these scenarios are unfortunate because just like a well-crafted chart can keep kids engaged in the writing process, so can a carefully placed mentor text. The question, then, is: How do you ensure that your kids use the mentor texts in your classroom as resources?

Imagine it's September. You want to include some mentor texts in your classroom for kids to use if they are having trouble coming up with topics. How can you do this in a way that really works? First, just as I suggested with charts, you should put out a limited amount of mentor texts—not too few, but not too many. Hopefully this will make the mentor texts more manageable to use. I might, for example, have a basket of five to seven books that the class has already read and/or talked about. I would clearly label this basket of books so that kids would know how these particular books might help them while writing. For example, there could be a basket of mentors labeled "Books to Go to When You're Unsure What to Write About." I might even include some sticky notes or index cards with some guiding questions as a further support system. For example, inside a nonfiction book about cats, I might include a sticky note (or index card) that says: "Does this book give you an idea of an animal that you know about or are interested in? That might be a good topic choice for you." This particular question would nudge kids to think about not just the topic of cats but the category of animals, which would open up a wider range of topic ideas.

Writing Centers Put Kids in Charge of Supplies

A writing center is an area in your classroom where kids can find the writing supplies they need. The goal of a writing center is to put the teacher out of the job of handing out supplies and put kids in the role of deciding what supplies and materials they need. I can remember being in one classroom where a teacher's writing center looked beautiful . . . for about a day. On the first day, she had out every single cool supply and material: revision paper, stapler, fancy pens, date stamp—you name it, she had it out. Although for a moment it looked good, the kids didn't use the writing center well because they didn't know what was there or understand the purpose of the materials.

I suggest you put out only the supplies you have already introduced. Also, consider having two smaller writing centers rather than one big one. Kids can get their supplies more quickly and spend more time writing rather than waiting in one big line at the writing center. Finally, I recommend that kids gather as many of the supplies as possible before writing workshop even begins. As a writer, I have my most productive writing days when I begin the day by gathering the supplies I think I'll need. It doesn't mean that something doesn't pop up while writing and I have to pause and go get it. But by thinking this through beforehand, I have fewer interruptions from my writing.

To a K–2 group, I might say, "Writers, before we gather for our focus lesson, I want you to think about what supplies you'll need today. Jan and Bill will pass your folders out so you can see where you left off yesterday. Are you starting a new piece? Does that mean you need new pages for a book? How many do you think you'll need? Or do you just need a booklet? Do you have a sharpened pencil? A marker? A revision pen? Perhaps you need revision paper today? All of these are good questions to consider. You have two minutes to read over your writing, make a plan for what you'll do today, and get the supplies you need. Meet me on the rug once you've done this."

To a grades 3–5 group, I might say, "Writers, before we gather for our focus lesson, I want you to think about what supplies you'll need today. Jan and Bill will pass out writer's notebooks and your rough draft folders. Are you working in your notebook? Are you drafting? If so, do you need more draft paper? Do you have a sharpened pencil? A revision pen? All of these are good questions to consider. You have two minutes to read over your writing, make a plan for what you'll do today, and get the supplies you need. Meet me on the rug once you've done this."

Figure 3.2 lists essential supplies for your classroom writing center.

Student Writing Samples Develop Resourcefulness

Another resource that kids can use is their classmates' writing samples. There is something magical about kids looking at and referring to one another's writing. A craft technique can seem less daunting if kids see it used by a classmate rather than an adult published author. When I went to South Street School, one of the

FIGURE 3.2 WRITING CENTER SUPPLIES

Supplies That You Will Eventually Want in Your Writing Center to Help Kids Be More Self-Directed

Pencils	"Boo boo tape" (cover-up tape) (K–2)
Revision pens	Editing pens
Blank pages to make a book with (K–2)	Date stamp
Ready-made booklets (K–2)	Different types of genre paper (K–2)
Rough draft paper (3–5)	
Different graphic organizers (3–5)	Writing folders (K–2)
Revision paper (K–2)	Writers' notebooks (3–5)

things that struck me was how often kids used other students' writing to help them. In these K–2 classrooms, writing was featured not on bulletin boards but at every table in plastic picture frames. The pieces that were displayed were not random; they were based on the focus lessons that week. The teachers used work by students who had tried what they'd taught. The writing samples were clearly labeled with the craft technique implemented, with the hopes that labeling them (and keeping them close by at writing tables) would make it easier for kids to use them as resources during the independent portion of writing workshop. If you are an upper-grade teacher and don't have tables in your classroom, you certainly could feature the writing on a bulletin board or in some other fashion around the room. The trick is to place it somewhere easily accessible and to label it in a way that helps kids understand how they might use it as a resource.

● Assess the Classroom Environment for Self-Directed Learning

In order to create a classroom that is conducive to self-directed learning, you'll want to periodically assess the effectiveness of it. In Figure 3.3, I've included an assessment system that you can use to reflect upon and tweak your classroom environment. I suggest that you use this assessment both when kids are interacting with the materials and when they are not. That way, you can really dig in deep and examine each part carefully.

FIGURE 3.3 CLASSROOM ENVIRONMENT ASSESSMENT

● A Close-In Look at Classroom Charts

Walk through your classroom or your colleague's classroom when there are no kids present and answer the following questions.

Are there process charts?

Are there craft charts?

Are there other charts (e.g., a word wall) that support kids?

How might these charts support kids in self-directed learning?

What are some potential issues you see with these charts? How could you solve them?

Now walk through your classroom or your colleague's classroom while kids are in the midst of writing workshop and answer the following questions.

Are kids using the charts? If so, how?

How are these charts helping kids to be self-directed?

If they are not using the charts, what could you do to change that?

Are there other issues? How can you solve them?

● A Close-In Look at the Writing Center

Walk through your classroom or your colleague's classroom when there are no kids present and answer the following questions.

What types of materials are there?

How are the materials stored?

How might these materials support kids in self-directed learning?

Are there potential issues you see with the writing center? How would you solve them?

Now walk through your classroom or your colleague's classroom while kids are in the midst of writing workshop and answer the following questions.

Are kids using the writing center? If so, how?

How is the writing center helping kids to be self-directed?

If kids aren't using the writing center, what could you do to change that?

Are there any other issues? How can you solve them?

FIGURE 3.3 CLASSROOM ENVIRONMENT ASSESSMENT, *CONT.*

● A Close-In Look at Mentor Texts

**Walk through your classroom or your colleague's classroom
when there are no kids present and answer the following questions.**

Are there mentor texts available for kids to use? What kinds?

How are they organized and labeled?

How might this support self-directed learning?

What are the potential problems? How could you solve them?

**Now walk through your classroom or your colleague's classroom while kids are
in the midst of writing workshop and answer the following questions.**

Are the kids using the mentor texts? If so, how?

How are the mentor texts helping kids to be self-directed?

If kids aren't using the mentor texts, what could you do to change that?

Are there other issues? How can you solve them?

● A Close-In Look at Student Writing

**Walk through your classroom or your colleague's classroom
when there are no kids present and answer the following questions.**

Is there student writing for kids to refer to?

How is it organized? Will it be easy for them to refer to during writing
workshop?

How might this support self-directed learning?

Are there potential problems? How could you solve them?

**Now walk through your classroom or your colleague's classroom while kids are
in the midst of writing workshop and answer the following questions.**

Are kids using student writing? If so, how?

How might this support self-directed learning?

If they are not using student writing, what could you do to change that?

Are there other issues? How could you solve them?

COLLABORATION IN ACTION:
STUDYING CLASSROOM ENVIRONMENTS

I had the wonderful opportunity to study classroom environments with first- and second-grade teachers at King Street Elementary School in Danbury, Connecticut. We studied their classroom environments in mid-September and used the questions in Figure 3.3 to guide our conversations.

The first thing we realized is that there was no way we could or should have all of these things in place in September. This realization reminded us that it is a misconception that getting kids to be self-directed is only September work. The major work of creating a classroom environment that is conducive to self-directed writers starts in September but continues throughout the year.

In some classrooms we saw examples of kids using process charts. Interestingly, kids were using the process charts that the teachers had modeled during focus lessons; they were not using the ones that the teachers had made quickly and just briefly reminded the kids to use. We also noticed that there were a lot more process charts than craft charts. Because the start of the year is so much about teaching kids the process of writing workshop, it made sense, but we also knew that the time had come to start creating some craft charts that would potentially help them to improve their writing. We also knew that we had to revisit some of the process charts that weren't being used and model how to use them.

In terms of mentor texts, there were actually a few kids using their independent reading books as mentor texts, but the main reason they were using them was to copy words. Although we were happy to see them using these texts as a way to solve problems during writing workshop, we wanted them also to use the texts as a way to lift the quality of their writing. This gave us plenty of food for thought on future work to do around mentor texts. We knew we had to model how to use mentor texts as a way to get craft ideas. We also realized that not only did we have to put more writing up in the room, but we also wanted to use some of our instructional time to model how to use the writing around the room to improve kids' writing.

● Additional Tips

Creating a classroom environment that is conducive for self-directed learning is not just a September project. I end this chapter with a few tips that you can use both in September and across the year to continue striving for the ideal classroom environment.

Don't Just Put the Resources Out—Model and Revise Them

Whether you are putting out a new mentor text, a new chart, new materials for the writing center, or a new piece of student work, you want to make sure that you linger for a bit on the new resource, modeling not only how you might use it, but also problems that might arise and how to solve those problems.

When I was a teacher and was introducing new resources to my kids, it sounded something like this: "So, kids, there is a new chart up about what to do when you think you are finished. Don't forget to use it if you need it." Because I felt rushed for time, I would just say something quickly about the resource and hope that the quick reminder would be enough. As you can probably guess, it was enough for a few of my kids, but for most it wasn't anywhere close to what they needed in order to be able to use the tool well. Most needed me to linger on it. Following is an example from a teacher who did just that.

Lorena Tesbir created a chart with her students about what to do if they thought they were finished writing. The chart had three options:

1. Reread your writing and add or change parts. (revision)
2. Reread your writing and check the spelling and punctuation. (editing)
3. Start a new piece of writing.

Before she put the chart up in the classroom, she pretended like she was a second-grade student who was finished. She then modeled reading the chart and choosing an option that was best for her. On a different day, she modeled some difficulty that she had in choosing the right option and then showed them how she solved the problem. Only after she had done those types of lessons a few times did she display the chart in the classroom. She also explicitly told the kids it was their job to use the chart to help them decide what to do when they thought they were finished. Because Lorena lingered on the new chart, her kids understood what was on that chart and how to use it. In turn, it boosted their confidence. Also, because Lorena paid attention to the chart, the kids valued it more.

This kind of careful teaching into a tool often isn't enough. You'll also want to revisit classroom resources over time and get your kids talking about which resources are working or not working so that you can improve upon them. In *Opening Minds*, Peter Johnston says, "We should teach children how to think together because more problems of substance aren't amenable to solutions by individual minds, they need the force of multiple minds" (2012, 97). Conversations where children think together about the resources in the room will not only help you understand whether or not the tools are working but also help you figure out new solutions when things are not working as well as you would like.

Also, when starting a new chart with kids, tell them that while they are working, they will probably come up with some other options to add to the chart. For example, I was in a fourth-grade classroom and Megan Hoey, the classroom teacher, was doing a lesson on how a writer knows which part of his memoir is important. During the focus lesson, she talked about and charted two elements that might stand out in their pieces: an important character that changed or an important event. She told the kids that as they read their memoirs that day, they might find that one of these two options should be the focus of their pieces, but they might also discover that some other aspect of their memoirs was the most important. Sure enough, during the share two more ideas were added to the chart. One little boy said that his important part was a combination of an important person and an event, and a second boy said that his important part was a meaningful object. The chart became even more useful because the kids knew that they played an important role in making sure the chart included all of their ideas.

Ensure That Your Classroom Is Clutter-Free

I once was walking through classrooms with a group of educators. When we got to one particular classroom, everyone became excited. It certainly was a beautiful environment. There was an abundant amount of writing supplies. There were lots of beautiful charts with wise words of advice. Student work hung from every corner in the room. While everyone raved, I was quiet because even though the classroom was beautiful and filled with many resources, I wondered if kids were truly able to find what they needed and use it to solve problems on their own. I brought this concern up to both the group and the classroom teacher. Upon reflection, the classroom teacher realized that most of the kids didn't use the classroom environment as well as she would have liked them to. We wondered if having a less cluttered classroom might help.

Earlier in this chapter I spoke about visiting classrooms at South Street School. While visiting, I was struck by how minimalistic the classrooms were. The only materials out were the ones that the kids were presently using. Materials that would be used later in the year and the teachers' materials were stored away. The teachers also knew that the charts that were up then might be taken down at some point to avoid clutter. These resources would not disappear from the classroom but would be kept in a less visible place so that kids who still needed them could access them.

Move Charts from Grade to Grade

Not only was I struck by how uncluttered the classroom environments at South Street School were, but I was also floored (and a little confused) by how resourceful the kids were so early in the year. My visit took place during the second week of school and there already were quite a few charts up and kids were using them as if they had been in school forever. I later discovered that the kids had used these very same charts the year before. Marnie Schork, the wise principal of this school, asked all of her teachers to have some (not all) consistent charts across the grades. At the end of the year, the teachers could pass along their charts to the teachers in the next grade. Teachers were then able to start the year with these familiar charts.

Often when kids start a new school year, it looks as though they have forgotten everything they learned the year before. Many times all it takes is a visual reminder such as a chart to jolt their memory. The familiar charts allowed the teachers to hit the ground running at the start of the year. Not only that, but the kids also were more confident and excited because their year started with what they already knew.

The visit to South Street School gave me a renewed vigor and a deeper understanding of the importance of classroom environments; they are not just a decoration or a September task. Strong classroom environments catapult kids into becoming more self-directed writers.

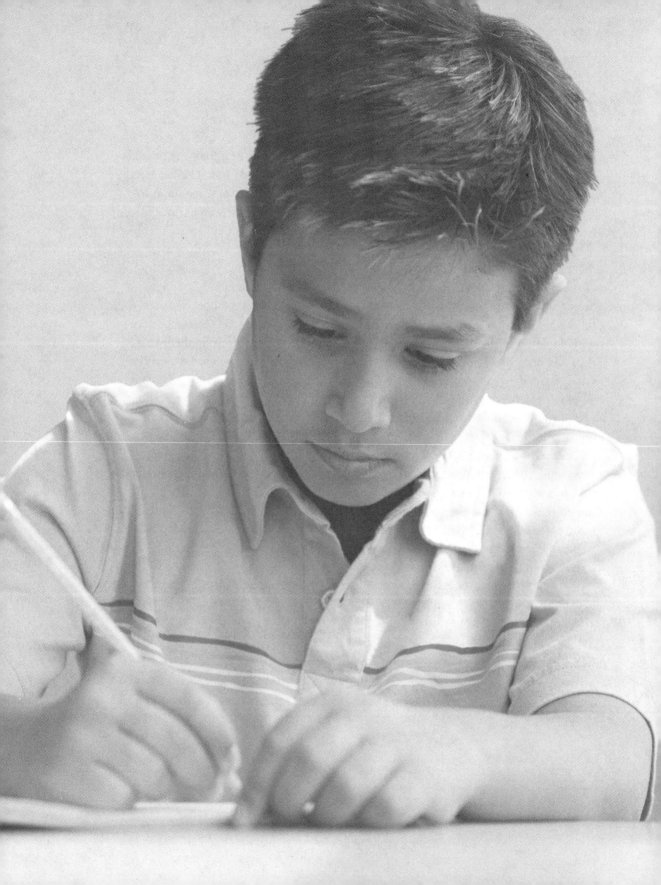

CHAPTER 4

> "We tend to view conflicts in the classroom as simply distractions from academic learning, so we try to eliminate them as quickly as possible by invoking our authority as teachers. This might get us back to academics more quickly, but at the cost of reducing the moral authority and commitment of the students."
>
> —PETER JOHNSTON, *OPENING MINDS*

MANAGING THE WRITING WORKSHOP TO SUPPORT SELF-DIRECTED LEARNING

I struggled with management throughout my first year of teaching. I had lofty ideas that year of what I wanted my kids to accomplish, but my goals were impossible to meet because I was unable to manage my kids in a way that enabled them to work independently. As a matter of fact, I found myself running around like a chicken from student to student, trying to put out fires and get the kids to do some work. I now realize that no lofty idea can be accomplished in any depth without some good old-fashioned classroom management.

In the previoius chapter, I spoke about how the classroom environment, if organized properly, can become a critical tool in helping students become more self-directed. In this chapter, I suggest that how the teacher manages the classroom is crucial as well. You'll learn some guiding management principles and helpful language as well as some rituals and routines that you can implement immediately to assist your students in becoming more confident, engaged, excited, and independent.

● Keep Kids Engaged by Establishing Consistent Celebrations

Lack of engagement is one of the primary factors that lead to management issues. Whenever I am working in a classroom, one of the first things I suggest to the teacher is to make sure he or she is having regular writing celebrations. Knowing there is a celebration coming up helps keep students engaged in the work at hand. By regular, I mean about one every three to four weeks, usually at the end of a writing unit of study. These celebrations don't always have to be fancy or time-consuming. While you can sometimes type up their writing pieces and invite parents, you can also, at times, celebrate by simply having the children read their final books or drafts to their reading buddies. As an added touch, you could have a cup of juice and a few crackers for each child to commemorate the occasion. They'll appreciate this kind of celebration just as much! What's important about any kind of celebration is that it's bigger than just putting the writing on the bulletin board. It should involve real readers and real audiences.

Once during a keynote speech, Mem Fox said, "Readers are what make writing matter." I wish I could say that I were the kind of person who writes no matter what, but the reality is that I'm not. I write when I know my purpose and my audience. I'm energized and self-directed when I have a deadline and an audience who is waiting to read my words. It's the same for our kids. If we want our kids to be energized and self-directed during writing workshop, we must continually give them deadlines and celebrations as anchors. Make sure you let students know about the deadline and celebration early on in the unit and then continue to mention them throughout the unit. If kids are aware of both the deadline and the celebration, they'll be much more likely to work hard and be committed to having a finished piece they'll be proud of.

⬤ Be Proactive: Encourage Kids to Be Independent First and Interdependent Second

When I was growing up, my dad used to say, "Hope for the best but be prepared for the worst." Although the negativity of that statement annoyed me to no end when I was a teenager, now that I'm an adult, I understand what he was trying to say. It's particularly helpful when thinking about classroom management. While you don't want to walk around your classroom worrying about every single worst-case scenario, you do want to think about some of the things that could go wrong during the independent phase of the writing workshop and then brainstorm possible solutions with your kids. If they don't happen, great, but if they do, you'll have solutions at your fingertips and be able to quickly suggest these solutions to your kids.

I saw this in action in Lorena Tesbir's second-grade classroom. At the end of her writing focus lesson, Lorena planned to have her kids think about what they were going to write and then turn and practice saying their ideas out loud to their neighbors. Because she thought about this beforehand, she knew there might be some kids who would say that they didn't know what to write about. Consequently, she was very deliberate in her language before she had them turn and talk. She said, "Now, if you are not sure what you're going to write about today, ask your partner to go first. I'm sure if you hear what he or she is writing about, it will help you think of a topic."

Sure enough, there were a few kids who didn't know what to write about, but they followed their teacher's advice. Because Lorena had given them a quick and easy solution before they experienced the problem, they felt empowered to solve the issue themselves. Imagine how differently this scenario would have gone if Lorena had said this instead: "If you don't know what to write about, stay behind after the lesson and I'll help you out." These seemingly harmless words would have actually prevented students from becoming more self-directed because instead of learning ways to solve problems by themselves (i.e., using their friends' ideas to spark their own ideas), they would have learned that in order to get unstuck, they needed to rely on the teacher.

I recommend that teachers, on a regular basis, think about the potential problems that might arise during writing workshop and then think of some possible solutions. Then they can do what Lorena did: try to give tips before the problems occur so that kids can solve them on their own rather than look toward others for solutions.

● Be Quiet So That Kids Realize They Can Solve Their Own Problems

While it's essential that you are proactive and try to solve problems before they occur, there will still be times when no matter how proactive you are, kids will be unable to solve problems on their own. Another important thing to keep in mind while managing your classroom is to make sure that you give children plenty of breathing space and thinking time with the hope, of course, that it will help them discover ways to solve problems themselves.

In *Quiet Leadership*, David Rock (2006) explains what happens in the brain when a person solves his own problems. A synapse forms in the brain. The brain builds a new map and it actually gets smarter. It's what we think of as a "lightbulb moment." Think of that high that you get when you figure out something that was once difficult. That's your brain building new maps, and it feels great! That's the same feeling that your kids will get if you stand back and let them solve problems on their own. When you jump in and solve a problem for them, you are unintentionally stealing that lightbulb moment from them.

Lorena, the teacher from the earlier example, had a child that still didn't know what to write about at the end of the turn-and-talk time. Instead of jumping in and helping him find a topic, she said, "Why don't you go back to your seat and give yourself a moment to think? I have a feeling that will help." The student went back to his seat and Lorena spent the first few minutes, as she always did, watching the kids but not talking to them.

Sure enough, when she went to check in with him after a few minutes of silence, he had thought of an idea and happily started to make his book. When she saw him working, she said to him, "Look at that. You thought you needed my help in solving this problem, but you solved it on your own." When he heard those words, his already beaming face beamed some more. Another synapse forming, another brain getting smarter. Again, this would have gone differently if Lorena had said right from the start: "You still don't have an idea. Didn't you go to your grandmother's house this weekend? Why don't you write about that?"

Lorena is comfortable with silence because she has seen countless times that her silence has enabled children to become more independent and thus more confident. Silence helps kids realize that they don't always need help from someone else but rather have the resources within themselves to solve problems and make decisions. What a high for them! Once a child solves one problem on her own, she is bound to become more comfortable with and confident in trying this again and again. Figure 4.1 illustrates the power that language can have to either promote independence or get kids to be more dependent on the teacher or other students.

Be Mindful of Which Problems You Solve for Kids and When

Just as there are times when teachers should be quiet and give kids thinking space, there are times when no matter how much thinking space we give them, they still need our help. In these situations, it's critical to think about the type of help you give and which problems you actually solve. Let me give you an example of what I mean. Let's say a student is struggling to come up with an idea even after you've given him some thinking time. You could sit and talk to that child and remind him of a topic or story that he could write about and then send him off—problem

FIGURE 4.1 LANGUAGE ANGLED TOWARD SELF-DIRECTED LEARNERS

Scenario	Say this . . .	Instead of this . . .
A child doesn't know what to write about.	Why don't you take a quiet moment to think? I'm sure you will come up with something.	You went to your grandmother's house this weekend. Why don't you write about that?
A child doesn't know what to do when he or she is finished.	How could you help yourself? (You might say this while pointing to a chart.)	When you are finished, come show me what you've done. *or* When you are finished, reread your piece. *or* When you are finished, start a new piece.
A child doesn't know how to spell a word.	How could you figure this out? (You might point to your mouth to give the hint of stretching it out.) *or* Where could you look? (You could point to the word wall.) *or* Let's say the sounds together.	Let me write that word down for you. *or* Listen to me say the sounds. Look at my mouth. *or* Ask a friend.

solved, right? Well, kind of. It's true that you would have solved his problem of not knowing what to write about, but the child wouldn't know how to solve it by himself next time. He would view himself as someone who needed his problems solved by someone else and would continue using you as a problem solver rather than become more self-directed. It would also take you away from being able to confer in more in-depth ways. You can't help kids improve the quality of their writing if you are just helping them come up with ideas. In reality, solving in this way only puts a bandage on a bigger problem.

Rather than just help the kid find a topic, I would share some strategies for how he could solve the problem of not knowing what to write about (reread old writing, think about topics that he knows a lot about, look at other books to get ideas) and then ask him to choose and use one of these strategies. Finally, I would end the conference by asking the child what he could do next time in order to solve the problem on his own.

Keep in mind that whatever the problem is ("I don't know what to write about" or "How do you spell . . . ?" or "I am finished. What should I do next?"), it will feel easier to solve the problem for the student and be done with it. I strongly recommend that you fight that instinct. Instead, slow down and teach kids how they can solve problems on their own.

● Be Flexible and Don't Forget the End Goal Is Self-Directed Writers

A friend of mine shared with me a revelation that she had about raising her two daughters. She had become accustomed to particular ways of speaking to her oldest child to resolve conflict. She kept using those ways because they worked. Eventually she realized that these same ways of speaking to Cameron, her oldest daughter, weren't working nearly as well with her younger daughter, Logan. Because the girls are different people with different needs and personalities, my friend had to figure out new ways to speak with Logan. In the beginning, my friend thought it was important to be consistent in how she spoke to both daughters, but she soon realized that rather than being consistent with how she spoke to them, she had to be consistent in what her end goal was for them. How she got to that goal of resolving conflict with each of her girls was going to be different.

No matter what you do, you are bound to have kids who are not doing as much as you would like during writing workshop. It's easy to attribute this to one single reason and then try to solve the problem the same way each time, just as my friend tried with her two daughters. It's important to be consistent in your end goal, just as my friend was, but you need to be open to having different paths on how you'll get there. In their book *Engaging Children's Minds: The Project Approach*, Katz and Chard (1989) conclude that a homogeneous curriculum leads to heterogeneous outcomes and if education systems want homogeneous outcomes, they will need to provide heterogeneous opportunities to learn.

It's important to remember that if you want to have a well-managed classroom where everyone is independent and engaged, you need to be able think outside the box and solve problems in different ways for different kids. To bring this idea to life, let me share the following story from a kindergarten classroom.

During a small moment unit of study, there was a student who, no matter what I did, got little or nothing accomplished during writing workshop. Whenever he was working by himself, basically all he did was fool around, bother other kids, and say he needed help. When I did work with him and tried to get him to tell me a small moment story from his life, he would inevitably start telling me everything he knew about dinosaurs.

I thought I was being clever by asking him questions such as: "Can you tell me about one time when you played with a dinosaur?" But he would still revert back to talking to me about dinosaurs in a way that was nowhere close to a small moment. To figure out how to help him, I had to first ask myself why he might be struggling. To me, he seemed to be struggling because he had no interest in writing a small moment story from his life. I realized that trying to get this child to write a small moment, at this point, was just not working and was not helping me reach my goal of getting him to be more engaged or more independent. I had to approach it differently with him, at least for now.

I decided not to worry about whether he was writing a small moment and focus more on getting him to write in a way that was engaging for him. That was a no-brainer. He clearly would be more engaged and independent if he were writing what he knew about dinosaurs. Even though the class was in a small moment unit of study, I showed him one of Gail Gibbons' nonfiction books and how she taught about a topic by drawing a picture and then labeling the parts of that topic. I let him know that he could do a similar thing: He could draw pictures and label the parts of dinosaurs. For the first time, I saw the glimmer in his eye. He was engaged and excited and independent while working on this new writing project. He shared with the class that day the dinosaur book he made, which built up his excitement and confidence even more. His behavior drastically changed after this. He went from someone who fooled around during writing workshop to someone who was usually far too busy making books to have time to fool around.

While he wasn't writing a small moment like the rest of the class was, he was much more engaged, confident, and independent, and he was able to write for longer periods of time. Did I want him to write in the genre that the class was studying? Of course I did, but one goal at a time is the only way that we can move writers. And the first goal for him had to be to help him become more self-directed by becoming more confident, engaged, and independent.

● Be Firm: Empower Kids to Become More Independent

Although it's important to be flexible and try to understand why a child is having difficulty, it's also important to know when to be firm. Writing workshop some-times gets a bad rep in the world for being a loose and unstructured time. There is nothing further from the truth. My first principal, Lesley Gordon, used to say that you should have a vision for how you want your classroom to look and sound and not deter from that vision until it occurs. In order to achieve the vision you have for writing workshop, you'll at times need to be firm (but kind) with your students. By being resolute and holding kids to a standard, you are letting them know that you believe they are fully capable of that standard. Your steadfastness will often be the key to helping kids realize that they are capable of more.

Often teachers ask me what I would do if a child didn't write during writing workshop. It's always a hard question for me to answer because I just wouldn't let that go on for very long. My expectations are that children will write every day. If they weren't I would take swift action. Here is how I would address it: First I would ignore it. Sure, a little surprising, but if you're trying to establish a well-managed classroom, you can't let one student derail you. I would keep going with what I had planned on doing that day during writing workshop. I want students to see that their actions are not changing my actions. Only at the end of writing workshop would I casually walk up to that child and say, "I see that you haven't written today. In first grade you have to write every day, so I need to figure out when you'll do this. The only time that you'll have today is during choice time [or some other beloved activity]."

I want to react not in an angry mode but rather in a realistic mode. Many kids, if this happens once, will make it their business never to let it happen again. If so, then you know your firmness worked. If it doesn't work on the first or second time, then it is not the right solution for this student. If it happens too often, writing will feel like a punishment, which is counterproductive, so it's time to find another tactic.

I might have a conversation with the student letting him know that writers make plans for how much they will write in any given day. Then I would ask the child to make a plan for how much he thinks he can get done by drawing a line on the page and then trying to write to that line. If this didn't work, I would need to investigate further why this child wasn't writing: Was she having trouble coming up with topics? Was spelling an issue? Whatever the issue was, I would then try to address that issue.

● Reflect on and Revise Your Management

I wish I could go back to that first year of teaching. I would manage my classroom differently because I now understand how careful and deliberate management supports kids in becoming more self-directed. I would now have regular celebrations. I would be proactive and uncover solutions to problems before they occurred. I wouldn't talk nearly as much so my students would have the breathing space they needed to try to solve their own problems. I would be flexible and firm. Most importantly, I would do all of this with an eye toward being self-directed.

Managing your classroom is not simple. It does not occur only at the start of the year. Getting students to be self-directed is a process that will require you to continually reflect upon the ways that you manage and organize your classroom. It's only through this process that you can get all students to be more self-sufficient and better equipped to handle the autonomy and choice inherent in a strong writing workshop.

COLLABORATION IN ACTION:
STUDYING SYSTEMS OF MANAGEMENT

I had the opportunity to work with a group of second-grade teachers at King Street Elementary School. We worked in Lorena Tesbir's classroom. We went into her room with the lens of management and used the assessment in Figure 4.2 to guide our conversation. Lorena had already worked hard to establish management. Most of her students were well managed, and now she just had to hone in on a few who still were having some issues. One of the students we looked at was Jayson. It was almost comical to watch him. I noticed that Madi, the little girl sitting next to him, got extra paper and after a few seconds I realized why. She was getting paper not only for herself but also for Jayson. When she gave him the paper, she asked him, "Do you have a pencil?" A few minutes later his shoe was untied, and I watched the assistant teacher tie his shoe for him; after that, Madi gently tried to get him to start working. Everybody in the room was working hard to get him engaged and he was doing very little to help himself. Finally, Lorena conferred with him. She was kind and talked him through some things. Their conversation helped him finally get started.

The group's conversation during our debriefing meeting focused on next steps for Jayson and how to ensure that he did more work and the people around him did less work. Although Lorena didn't feel as though she was having quite enough celebrations, she did not think that more would necessarily help Jayson. She felt that she had to make sure that she was kind but firm with him. She had a distinct feeling that the next day he would not continue doing the work they had agreed upon. She knew she would have to be firm and hold him to what he agreed to do. If he didn't, she would have to let him know that they would need to find a time during the day when he could do it. Through our conversation we realized that the solution would be different depending on the kid. For some kids, celebrations are a great management tool. For others, a quiet time to think or an out-of-the-box solution might be necessary. The conversation helped us to tailor a solution that was just right for Jayson.

FIGURE 4.2 CLASSROOM MANAGEMENT ASSESSMENT

● What Management Problems Are You Having?

Do you have regular celebrations? If not, would regular celebrations help you solve some management problems?

How could you talk to kids in ways that would raise the level of engagement in your classroom?

Are you proactive? If not, are there things you could say or do to prevent a problem from happening in the first place?

When you see a problem, do you jump in or do you watch to see if and how the child attempts to solve it on his or her own?

What concrete ways have you tried to solve a problem? Are your solutions moving kids toward being more engaged and independent? If not, what could you do differently?

Does your problem need a flexible solution? If so, what could it be? Does your problem need you to be kind but firm? If so, what could you say?

CHAPTER 5

"When one puts up a building one makes an elaborate scaffold to get everything into its proper place. But when one takes the scaffold down, the building must stand by itself with no trace of the means by which it was erected. . . ."

—ANDRES SEGOVIA, MUSICIAN

THE ROLE OF SCAFFOLDED INSTRUCTION IN CREATING SELF-DIRECTED WRITERS

A few years ago, a spectacular park was being built in Hoboken (the town where I live) and my four-year-old nephew, Vince, was eagerly awaiting its completion. While the park was being built, I was able to catch a glimpse of the main slide. It was huge and I had a sinking feeling in my stomach that my nephew would take one look at it and burst into tears. Sure enough, when the park was finally completed and my nephew saw the slide, he cried with disappointment because he was sure he would be unable to climb up the long staircase and go down the slide by himself. My reaction: I wanted to hug him and let him know that he didn't have to do it and perhaps when he was older he could try. My sister-in-law's reaction was quite different. Anne said, "You'll be able to do it. Don't worry; I'll go up with you." Vince instantly felt reassured because he knew he wouldn't be alone on the slide.

Anne crouched down under Vince while he climbed the staircase so that if he slipped she would be right there to catch him. She also went down the slide with him on her lap. As time went on, he became more skilled and confident on the slide. Anne was able to support him less and less until finally he was able to get over his fear, take the risk, climb the staircase, and go down the slide all by himself!

Watching my sister-in-law, I realized how different our two reactions were. My reaction to have him wait because he wasn't ready could have increased his fear and held him back from doing something he actually could do. The reality was that he could do it but just needed some temporary support in order to become a more skilled and confident slide rider. By giving him the support, Anne was able to boost his confidence so that he would take a risk and realize that he could actually go down the slide. Not only that, but after she scaffolded his sliding he was willing to try other things on his own. Many of our students will need similar types of support in order to become more skillful, confident writers as well as greater risk takers.

This chapter explains that if you want all kids to become more self-directed, you need to provide them with writing support rather than hold them back from what you might view as too difficult. I begin by exploring what the word *scaffold* means in education. Then I share how we can use the different writing components to scaffold students. Finally, I delve into two of the writing components that you can use to scaffold student learning: (1) write-aloud and (2) interactive and shared writing. You'll learn what these two components look and sound like and how you can use them both inside and outside the writing workshop as temporary supports to nurture your students into becoming independent, confident writers and risk takers. You'll also hear the stories of teachers and see the writing samples of kids who have tried this work out in their classrooms.

● What Does It Mean to Scaffold Students?

Very often in education we hear about the importance of scaffolding our students. But what does that really mean? R. Keith Sawyer describes scaffolding as "a learning design to promote deeper learning" (2006). He further goes on to say that scaffolding is "the support given in the learning process, which is tailored to the needs of the students with the intention of helping the student achieve his/her learning goal. These supports are gradually removed as students develop autonomous learning strategies, thus promoting their own cognitive, affective and psychomotor learning skills and knowledge" (2006).

Brush and Saye (2002) describe two types of scaffolding: soft and embedded scaffolding and hard scaffolding. Soft scaffolding is support that is dependent upon the needs of the student in any given moment. It is not planned ahead of time. It happens in the moment. For example, Anne, my sister-in-law, didn't know that she was going to model for my nephew how to keep his eyes looking up toward the next bar as he climbed up the staircase for the slide. She did this only after she saw him looking down toward the ground while climbing.

Hard scaffolding is the type of support that you plan for ahead of time. For example, in Marnie Gleissner's classroom, some students were having a hard time with the structure of how-to (procedural) books. For these students, she created paper that would help them remember the different components. Specifically, the paper included a place for materials and then a place for the steps. This paper was a hard scaffold because she created the paper ahead of time. She hoped that after those students used this paper for a bit of time they would have a better understanding of the parts of a how-to and would eventually no longer need that paper.

How Can We Use the Writing Components to Scaffold Student Learning?

One way to help students become more self-directed is to put scaffolds in place. The goal is that when these scaffolds are removed, kids will have the confidence and skills they need to do the work independently. Scaffolds in writing often occur in the form of writing components. So what are the different writing components and how can they be used to scaffold learning?

Often, writing components are defined by the type of hard scaffolding they provide. For example, in *Writing Essentials*, Regie Routman defines shared writing as work in which "the teacher and students compose collaboratively, the teacher acting as expert and scribe for her apprentices as she demonstrates, guides and negotiates the creation of meaningful text, focusing on the craft of writing, as well as the conventions" (2005, 83). In her definition, the type of support given is not planned in the moment but decided beforehand. Likewise, in their book *Guided Reading*, Irene Fountas and Gay Su Pinnell talk about types of writing that are once again differentiated by the level of support given (1996, 23).

Although providing planned (or hard) scaffolding during the different writing components is important, I have also found that it's essential to offer support based on the immediate needs of your students (soft scaffolding). Rather than define the components by the level of support given, I tend to define them by the type of writing skills or strategies taught.

● Two Writing Components That Scaffold Student Learning

The two writing components that I believe scaffold student learning are (1) interactive and shared writing and (2) write-aloud. I tend to use interactive and shared writing as ways to focus on the conventions of writing, and I use write-aloud as a way to focus on the craft of writing. If you think about it, reading instruction is often organized in this manner. Read-aloud is focused on the comprehension of reading and shared reading is focused more on the conventions of reading.

Here is a list of some of the skills that you might want to teach your kids and which component (write-aloud or interactive and shared writing) is more suitable:

- decide upon a topic: write-aloud
- decide upon a genre (when not writing in a particular genre): write-aloud
- experiment with more complicated sentence structures: write-aloud
- ensure that sentences are grammatically correct: interactive and shared writing
- spell sight words correctly: interactive and shared writing
- use what you know about letters, sounds, and words to spell words the best you can: interactive and shared writing
- use punctuation correctly: interactive and shared writing

In the following sections, first I define each of the components. Then, I show the component in action in a teacher's classroom. After that, I discuss the teacher's role in ensuring that it is successful as well as how to use the component to promote self-directed learning.

Write-Aloud

During a keynote speech at the Literacy for All Conference in 2009, Lester Laminack said the following about the importance of students reading well-crafted picture books: "Students need to put it together with their mouths before they put it together with their hands." While he was addressing the importance of students reading well-crafted picture books, he could have just as easily been talking about write-aloud. Write-aloud gives all students the opportunity to put well-crafted pieces together with their mouths so that it's easier for them to get the writing down with their hands later during the independent writing portion of writing workshop.

During write-aloud, the teacher and students compose a piece of writing together around a shared topic. By shared, I mean a topic, a story, or an idea about which the students have either exactly the same or almost the same knowledge as that of the teacher. It could be a story based on an event that has occurred in the classroom or a class field trip, or it might be information about a common topic such as the school or a class pet. It could also be a shared idea such as advocating for more recess time or better school lunches. It should *not* be a story, an idea, or an informational topic that only the teacher knows about, because the kids can't contribute to the writing in any meaningful way. Don't feel like you need an exciting story, fancy information, or some unique idea in order to do this. As a matter of fact, I have found the simplest topics are often the best. One teacher I worked with did some fabulous work with her kindergarten class about a time when she spilled juice during snack time. It was powerful because the topic was focused, simple, and important to the kids.

The goal of write-aloud is not the mechanics of writing (that's the role of shared and interactive writing), but rather the composition of writing. During write-aloud, students listen to and watch the teacher as she writes aloud and notices aloud her use of composition and thinking strategies. Most importantly, the students join the teacher in the writing process. They think and then practice out loud different types of sentence structures. The hope, of course, is that this out-loud composition work serves as a stepping-stone for students to do similar work in their own writing.

To get an idea of what write-aloud looks and sounds like in the classroom, let's look at a snippet of one that took place in Trisha O'Brien's third-grade classroom. In this particular write-aloud, we were planning and developing the main character, Samantha, for a short fiction study. The day before, we had brainstormed different words to describe Samantha. After this initial brainstorming session, I made the decision that Samantha would be bossy even though she secretly yearned for friends. I insisted that the fictional character Samantha was eight (the same age as most of the students) so the students could use their shared knowledge about being eight to help them write.

LEAH: Today we're going to begin developing Samantha, the main character. We're going to think of some of the things she might do if she truly is bossy but wants friends. For example, if she is bossy, I could imagine this sentence in the story: "Samantha grabbed all of the pencils from the middle of the table." That shows she is bossy, doesn't it? I don't know if that exact sentence will end up in our story, but it makes sense, right?

Now, you're going to try what I just did. Turn and talk to the person next to you and practice aloud some action sentences that would make sense in our story about bossy Samantha.

[As the students turn and talk, I conduct mini conferences with different partnerships, helping them structure different types of action sentences.]

LEAH: Let's share some of your action sentences.

BILL: Samantha pushed kids out of the way because she wanted a pony poster.

LEAH: That sentence would really make sense in a chapter titled "The Book Fair." Perhaps Samantha and her class are attending a book fair and Samantha sees a poster and, being the bossy girl that she is, pushes her friends Emily and Katie out of the way because she thinks she should have the poster. Listen to the sentence again: "Samantha pushed kids out of the way to try to get to the poster first." Did I say your sentence correctly, Bill?

BILL: Yes.

LEAH: Would that make sense? Does that show she's a bit bossy? *[Kids start yelling out, "Yes!"]* Turn to a neighbor, and let's practice this part of the story using some action words. Perhaps the story would start something like this: "One fall morning Ms. Miller's class was very excited. They could not stop looking at the clock because they knew at 10:15 they were going to the book fair. Finally the time came and Samantha and her class walked down the hall to the book fair. When they walked in, there was a big beautiful pony poster." What kinds of actions might happen next with our character Samantha? Practice the exact words aloud as you imagine how they might sound in that chapter. You can try out Bill's action sentence there or you can invent your own action sentence.

[As students turn and talk, I conduct mini conferences to scaffold students' attempts.]

LEAH: Let's have some kids practice some of their action sentences out loud.

PETER: Samantha pushes Emma and Katie away and runs toward the poster with money in her hand to buy it.

LEAH: Would that make sense? Say Peter's idea to a partner. Does it make sense?

[I jot notes in my notebook as kids practice Peter's sentence.]

LEAH: Anyone else?

KARA: Samantha sees a beautiful pony poster. She doesn't want anyone else to have it, so she pushes her friends Emma and Katie out of the way so that she can be the first in line to buy it.

PAUL: Samantha sees a pony poster she's always wanted. She pushes her friends Emma and Katie out of the way and says, "Get out of my way! That pony poster has my name written on it." *[I continue to jot notes in my notebook so that I don't forget the sentences they are saying.]*

LEAH: Interesting, Paul. You practiced not only what Samantha might do if she is bossy but also what she might say. Some of these sentences could very well end up in our class story. I'm writing all of your ideas in my notebook and will later put them on our planning page.

THE TEACHER'S ROLE DURING WRITE-ALOUD

- Notice how I started the write-aloud session by modeling a structurally complex sentence. This gave students an example of what they were about to try. Across the write-aloud session, I modeled and asked kids to try out new types of sentence structures.
- Notice how I asked the children to say entire sentences out loud rather than single words. Because of this request, the children were practicing saying more complex sentences, which hopefully would lead to writing more complex sentences in the future. This type of oral practice is beneficial to all students, but it is especially beneficial to English language learners.
- Notice how I conferred with different kids during the session, scaffolding them as they practiced these different types of sentence structures. I decide whom to confer with depending upon what I know about each student and the type of scaffolding I believe he or she will need.
- I also make sure that everyone participates rather than just my strongest kids. Whenever I do write-aloud and someone tries out an interesting

sentence, I have the rest of the kids turn to their partners and practice either that exact sentence or one that is similar to it.

- Instead of making a chart, I took notes on what kids were saying so I could make the chart later. When I don't make the chart right there on the spot, I can focus my attention on the main job of write-aloud, which is to get every student to practice new and varied sentence structures. It doesn't mean that making a chart in the midst of write-aloud is inherently wrong. It just takes many teachers away from the more important job of helping all students practice different types of sentences aloud. Some teachers who have a coteacher or an assistant might have one teacher making the chart while the other works with students on practicing literary language.

HOW TO USE WRITE-ALOUD IN THE CLASSROOM TO PROMOTE SELF-DIRECTED LEARNERS

- Write-aloud can be conducted as a whole group, separate from the writing workshop. Many teachers have a sacred time for read-aloud every single day, when they have kids practice the type of comprehension that they'll eventually do while reading independently. Why wouldn't we have a sacred time for write-aloud when kids practice the type of composing that they'll eventually do while writing independently during writing workshop? Including this type of scaffold on a regular basis enables kids to get the support they need when learning new skills and strategies, which in turn increases their confidence. Increased confidence means kids are willing to take more risks when composing in different genres.
- You can use write-aloud at the start of a writing unit of study to support immersion. As you'll see in Chapter 7, I suggest that many writing units of study start with immersion. Immersion has two components: one is for kids to study mentor texts that are written in the same genre and the second is for the teacher to conduct a write-aloud in the genre. Doing this first will give kids the confidence and skills they need when approaching that genre independently during writing workshop. Kids who are really struggling might choose to model their first independent piece after the write-aloud. It could be the starting point they need to become engaged in the writing process. Many teachers will turn the write-aloud into a class chart that children can refer to throughout the study.

- You can use write-aloud as your method of teaching in your focus lessons. Many people also use the write-aloud that the class made later on during the study as a vehicle to teach important concepts. For example, I could conduct a focus lesson on effective beginnings by using the piece created during write-aloud. More than likely I would both model and ask kids to revise the write-aloud by trying out the types of beginnings I was teaching.

- You can use write-aloud as a method of teaching in your conferences. Many teachers already use mentor texts as a teaching method in their conferences. Your write-aloud can now serve as an additional mentor text. When you use the write-aloud in both focus lessons and conferences, it is often even more powerful than mentor texts written by published authors because the kids are the creators of these texts and therefore they feel more childlike and less intimidating.

- You can use write-aloud as your method of teaching during small-group instruction. During reading workshop, we often pull kids together for guided reading. We choose a text. We give it a proper book introduction and then we ask all of the kids to read that book. We do that with the hopes that our book introduction will give kids a challenging but successful reading experience. Why not do the same types of things during writing workshop? Write-aloud is the perfect vehicle for guided writing. You can gather a group of kids together with your class write-aloud in hand. You can remind them of all of the previous work done with this piece and perhaps talk a bit more about it so that kids are properly introduced to the topic, story, or idea. Then you can ask each of them to write their own version of the write-aloud. The goal for guided writing would be similar to the goal for guided reading: scaffolding kids so that they have a successful and challenging writing experience.

During writing workshop, you'll want to look for evidence that the write-aloud is helping kids in positive ways. Figure 5.1 has some questions that might help.

FIGURE 5.1 WRITE-ALOUD ASSESSMENT

● Write-Aloud Assessment

Are some kids using the write-aloud for both the topic and the structure and craft? Is this helping them, or are they depending too heavily on the scaffold?

How will you move those students to using the write-aloud only for the structure and craft and not for the topic?

Are there some students who are not using the write-aloud to support their independent writing? Should they be? If so, what you can do to facilitate this?

COLLABORATION IN ACTION:
A WRITE-ALOUD

I worked with Marnie Gleissner and her first-grade students on using the write-aloud in the classroom as a scaffold. Marnie started her how-to (or procedural) unit of study by showing the kids some mentor texts as well as conducting a write-aloud. The topic of the class write-aloud was how to make an acorn picture frame. Before we went into the classroom, Marnie expressed a very wise concern. She wanted the how-to that the class would create to be a scaffold for the different learners in the classroom. Specifically, she was concerned that some students would rely too heavily on the write-aloud and write their how-to pieces using the same topic (how to make an acorn picture frame). On the other hand, she had some ELLs who she thought would benefit from writing a first how-to using both the topic and the structure and craft of the class write-aloud. She also worried that some kids would not use it enough. She thought they would go write their how-to pieces and not use any of the things they had learned while writing one together.

She kept her concerns in mind while creating her focus lesson for that day. Specifically, she modeled how she used the write-aloud to compose a new how-to. This piece was about how to play a particular math game in the classroom. While composing, she kept showing them how she used the structure and craft of the story about the acorn picture frame to help herself structure and craft her new how-to. She kept reminding her students that she chose a new topic but she used the write-aloud for ideas on how to structure and craft it. She nudged them to do the same thing.

It was interesting to note that Frank was the only student in the class who used the whole-class topic. Frank was an ELL and Marnie and I agreed that he made a wise choice. Using the whole-class topic gave him more language support. This led us back to our original conversation about how the write-aloud should serve not just as a scaffold but also as an appropriate scaffold for everyone. Because different kids used it differently, we were seeing this idea come to fruition. Frank's writing is in Figure 5.2. As you can see, the write-aloud was a true scaffold for him; he was able to compose the parts of a how-to by trying it out on the class write-aloud topic. The next step for him would be to have that same comfort level when writing on a topic of his choice.

FIGURE 5.2 FRANK'S HOW-TO PIECE (GRADE 1)

Introduction

Do you want to make a cuol Acorn Frame? then read my Book!

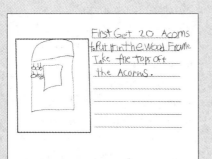

What You Need

4 Acorn tops   2 acorns   School Glue

1 Paper Plate   ribbon   1 wood Frme

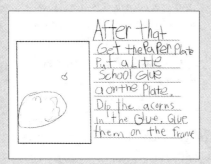

First Get 20 Acorns tu Put tin the wood Frame Take the Tops off the Acorns.

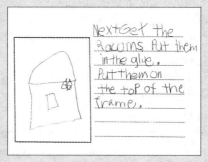

then Get the School Glue.

School Glue

After that Get the Paper Plate Put a Litle School Glue a on the Plate. Dip the acorns in the Glue. Glue them on the Frame

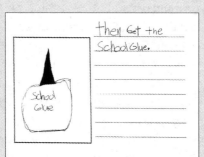

Next Get the 2 acorns Put them in the glue. Put them on the top of the Frame.

Last Get the ribbon and glue it on top.

Finally Get a new wood Frame to Put your Pitchr in!

you

Looking around the room, we also noticed that some kids chose giant topics such as how to be a good big brother or how to play football. We knew these topics would prove to be challenging, so we wondered if we should pull together a small group the next day and use the write-aloud to remind them that they could choose small, everyday school topics and rituals. It was interesting to note that when we gathered those kids the next day, half of them had already narrowed their topics on their own. In Figure 5.3 you can see Joselin's writing. Joselin had much more success when she chose an everyday ritual (how to unpack for school). Marnie, her teacher, was more easily able to confer with her, too, since she also knew the steps of how Joselin unpacked for school.

I also conferred with Catherine that day. As she wrote, she actually wasn't using the write-aloud as a scaffold at all, although I thought she should. In our conference, I showed her how she could use the displayed write-aloud to give her ideas on transition words. Sure enough, after that conference, she included them in her piece about how to tie shoes (see Figure 5.4).

FIGURE 5.3 JOSELIN'S WORK ON UNPACKING FOR SCHOOL (GRADE 1)

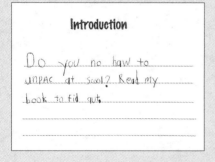

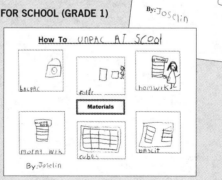

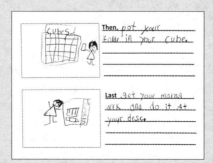

FIGURE 5.4 CATHERINE'S PIECE ON TYING SHOES (GRADE 1)

How To Tiy Shoos

By: Catherine

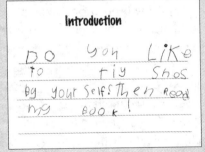

Introduction

DO you LiKe TO Tiy Shos By your Self. Then Read my BooK!

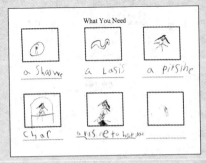

What You Need

a Shoow   a Lasis   a pitsihe

char   a kis re to help you

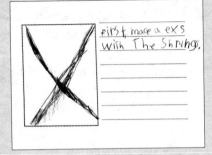

First mace a exs with The Shrihgs.

Next polle The String Til.

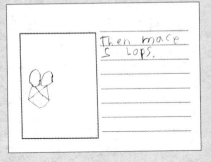

Then mace s lops.

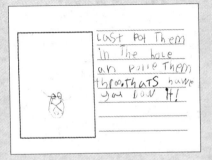

Last pot Them in the hole an polle Them throo.thats have you bow it!

Now you can Tiy your own Shoows!

Shared and Interactive Writing

Whereas write-aloud is a scaffold for craft, shared and interactive writing are scaffolds for the conventions of writing (punctuation, spelling, and phonics). During shared and interactive writing, the teacher comes up with both the idea and the language the kids will use while writing that idea. Once the teacher has shared this with the class, the teacher and kids write the message together, focusing on conventions such as spelling and punctuation. If the teacher is the one writing the words, then it is shared writing. If the teacher hands the pen to a student and asks him or her to write a part of a word or sentence, then it is interactive writing. If the teacher asks all the kids to write a part of the piece on a dry-erase board, it is still interactive writing. Generally any one session might include shared and interactive writing. A teacher who has a balance of both shared and interactive writing as well as write-aloud is more able to support her students in the many skills and strategies they need to become better, more confident writers.

To get an idea of what shared and interactive writing look like, let's visit a third-grade classroom where I am conducting a shared/interactive writing lesson. The principal had written a letter to the class asking the kids if they thought they were responsible enough to help out at the kindergarten picnic. The class was writing a letter back to the principal in response to her question.

LEAH: So, children, today we're going to write Ms. B. back to let her know that we do think we're responsible enough to help out with the kindergarten picnic. Yesterday, I overhead some of you saying that you have already proven that you're responsible enough to help out at the kindergarten picnic because, as book buddies, you already make sure that the kindergarten students read the entire time and don't get too silly. I think in our response letter back we should say that. I'm thinking we could write, "Dear Ms. B., We think that we are responsible enough to help out with the picnic because during book buddy time, we make sure the kindergarten students read the entire time without getting silly." I've already written, "Dear Ms. B." I've also written the start of the next sentence, "We think that we are," because most of you are spelling those types of words correctly and pretty easily while writing. If you are having any trouble with any of that, no worries. Take a moment now to look at those words and get them in your brain because the more that you look at them and get them in your brain, the easier it will be to spell and write them quickly. We're going to slow down and focus on the word *responsible*. One of the things we've been working on as a class is when we get to a long word, we slow down and listen across the word for all the parts that we know, rather than just the beginning sounds. Let's try the word *responsible* together. Say the word in your head and think about the parts that you know. Then turn and talk to someone about the parts that you know. [*The students do this.*] Who wants to say some of the parts that you know?

BILL: "Re."

LEAH: Does that come at the start or the end of the word?

CLASS: Start.

LEAH: Turn to someone near you and think about what letters you would use to represent "re." [*Students discuss their ideas.*] I heard many of you saying *r-e.* I'm going to go ahead and write that because that is the first chunk in this word. [*I write "re."*] Let's read this part. [*I point to the chunk "re" on the page.*] Respon. Is there a chunk or a part that you hear next?

SARA: "Spon."

LEAH: I hear that, too. It's not a word, but I bet if we work together we can figure out what letters we might use to represent that. Listen to the blend at the start of "spon." Say it out loud. What do you think it might be?

JOSE: S-*p* and then the word *on.*

LEAH: Let's put that together. We have the *re* and then the blend *sp* and then the word *on.* Sara, can you come up and write that? [*Sara comes up and adds "spon."*]

LEAH: Now we have "respon" and we have to keep working at this longer word until it says "responsible." This is when many of you tucker out and just write anything at the end. What I want you to do instead is to listen closely to what you hear at the end and write the letters that correspond. Listen especially closely to the vowel. After you say the word in your head, turn and share what you think this last chunk might be. [*The students do this.*] Tayla, what do you think it might be?

TAYLA: S-*a-b-l.*

LEAH: Sometimes we say the word a certain way and it sounds like it could be an *a*, but listen to how I'm saying the word. [*I say "sible" out loud.*]

TAYLA: *S-i.*

LEAH: What else might be in this chunk?

KIERA: *B* and *l*.

LEAH: There is a *b* and an *l*. I'm going to write that down. Now here is when I check to see if the word looks right. Ask yourself that question in your head. There are some murmurs of both yes and no. To me, it actually doesn't quite look right yet. There is one more letter at the end. What letter do you think might belong at the end to make this word look right?[*A few kids say,* "E."]

LEAH: It actually is *e*. Look at how we didn't get overwhelmed or intimidated by this big word. I notice that when writing, some of you start off strong and then write almost anything for the middle and the end of the word. Today we slowed down and asked ourselves about the parts that we knew across the entire word. Also at the end, we asked ourselves if the word looked right. You can do the exact same type of work when you write on your own during writing workshop. I'm going to finish this sentence by writing "enough to help out with the picnic" and we're going to work together on the next word in the sentence: *because*. *Because* is one of those words I just want you guys to know how to spell without even having to look at a word wall or trying to stretch it out. If that is our goal, where can we look in the room to help us make a permanent picture of that word in our brain?

BILL: The word wall under *B*.

LEAH: Let's find it. What do you notice about the word *because*? [*The kids share what they notice.*] On your dry-erase board, write that word a few times and make a picture of that word in your head. [*I give the kids time to do this.*] Who wants to come write it up here? Tom, come on up. [*Tom writes "because."*] *Because* is one of those words I just want you to know and be able to write quickly during writing workshop. Hopefully the work that we did together just now will help you to achieve that goal. I'm going to finish up this sentence and then we'll be just about ready to send our response letter back to Ms. B.

THE TEACHER'S ROLE DURING SHARED AND INTERACTIVE WRITING

- Notice how we didn't talk about every single part of the letter that we were writing to Ms. B. There were parts that I just wrote quickly with very little conversation as well as parts that I lingered on. All of these decisions were based upon my assessments of those particular students and what they needed to work on. In this case it was listening across longer and more sophisticated words as well as building a larger sight word vocabulary. There were also some assessment-based interactions occurring in the midst of this session. Tom, for example, often misspelled *because* in his writing, and I had a sense that if he just slowed down and pictured it, I could help him change this habit. Therefore, choosing Tom to write the word *because* was very purposeful. Also, at times during this session and other sessions I skipped over something not because the kids didn't need it but simply because it would be too much for this particular session. I try to keep shared and interactive writing short and sweet and save some of the teaching opportunities for future sessions.

- Notice how I made sure that everybody participated in the writing and the conversations. I did this in a few ways. First, there were quite a few turn-and-talk moments. Second, I had some kids come up and actually write parts of the letter. Third, there were times when everyone tried the work out on a dry-erase board.

HOW TO USE SHARED AND INTERACTIVE WRITING TO PROMOTE SELF-DIRECTED LEARNERS

- You can use shared and interactive writing with the whole group, separate from the writing workshop. Many teachers have a sacred time for shared reading in their weekly schedules to work on the conventions of reading. Why wouldn't we have a sacred time for shared and interactive writing when we support kids by focusing on the conventions of writing? Getting this type of writing support on a regular basis is bound to help kids become both confident and skilled in the different writing conventions. It will also support them to take on more risks while using conventions.

- You can use shared and interactive writing as your method of teaching. Many people use a shared or interactive writing piece that was composed with their class later during the study as a method of teaching. For example, if I had continued teaching in that third-grade classroom, I could have used the class writing piece that we had created to remind kids about how to take a big word and make it less intimidating by listening to the parts, just as we did with the word *responsible*. I could also use that same text to remind kids about the importance of knowing how to write certain words quickly (such as *because*). I could teach either of these things in whole-class focus lessons, one-on-one conferences, or small groups, depending on what my class or individual kids needed. Just as the class write-aloud can be used as a mentor text during one-on-one conferences, so can the shared or interactive writing piece.

● Scaffolds Are an Important Part of the Self-Directed Learning Puzzle

Giving students consistent and focused scaffolds is another way to ensure that all students become more self-directed writers. As you put all of the pieces of the puzzle together, you'll see all your learners become more and more self-directed.

> "Four steps to achievement: Plan purposefully.
> Prepare prayerfully. Proceed positively.
> Pursue persistently."
>
> —WILLIAM A. WARD, AUTHOR

CHAPTER 6

PLANNING A YEARLONG CURRICULUM THAT EMPHASIZES SELF-DIRECTED LEARNING

Typically when teachers create a yearlong plan for the teaching of writing, they plan what genres, skills, and strategies they will teach and when in the year they'll teach them. These days, many teachers are also thinking about the Common Core State Standards and how to ensure that their yearlong plans both address and exceed what those standards ask for. All of this is important, but it's not enough.

Not only do you want to create a yearlong plan that addresses content, but you also want to create a year that helps all kids become more self-directed. In this chapter, I explain some key ideas to keep in mind when planning for a year of self-directed learning. You'll read about the planning conversations that I had with the kindergarten and fifth-grade teams at PS 230 in Brooklyn, New York and see the curriculum calendars that we created based upon these conversations.

As I planned curriculum calendars with the teachers at PS 230, we focused on how to create plans that would support self-directed learners. Three big ideas guided us in achieving this goal:

1. Plan for a year that not only teaches kids new genres but also gives kids plenty of practice in these genres.
2. Plan for a year that gets kids to use what they have learned not only during previous units of study but also during previous years.
3. Plan for a year that connects reading and writing.

The Kindergarten Curriculum Planning Meeting

In Figure 6.1, you'll see the final kindergarten curriculum calendar that the kindergarten team at PS 230 and I created. This calendar was angled toward nurturing self-directed learners.

Plan for a Year That Teaches New Genres and *Gives Kids Plenty of Practice in Them*

Often when I visit schools and look at teachers' curriculum calendars, I notice they have decided upon the different genres that they will teach and in what month they'll teach each one. For each of these units, teachers generally plan to have kids bring one piece to publication. In the past, this is exactly how the teachers at PS 230 created their curriculum calendars, but Sharon Fiden, the school principal, wanted this to change. Although she knew it was important to teach new genres, she worried that kids were not getting enough practice with these genres since they published only one piece per unit and then moved on to a new genre the following month. One of her goals was for teachers to create curriculum calendars that would allow kids to have multiple opportunities to practice in the different genres. I was thrilled to hear her say this because the

FIGURE 6.1 KINDERGARTEN CURRICULUM CALENDAR

Kindergarten
September: Quick Publish and Launching the Writing Workshop
October: Observing, Talking, and Labeling
October–November: Illustration Study
December: Assessment-Based Unit
January: Writing for Many Purposes
February: All About Books
March: Assessment-Based Unit
March–April: Writing Stories with a Focus on Authors as Mentors
April–May: Opinion Books
June: Informational Writing (Shared Research)

more practice kids get in writing in the different genres, the more confident they will be.

With Sharon's input, the kindergarten teachers and I came up with two different ways to revise the calendars to ensure that kids got practice in the genres being taught. First, we decided to ask kids to publish multiple pieces during a unit of study, rather than just one. This was easy to imagine in kindergarten since kids were already creating multiple drafts in their folders. Now, it was just a matter of showing them how to do more revision and editing to these drafts.

Second, we decided to have some units of study that were not genre based but focused on particular skills and strategies. We called these assessment-based units because we did not decide ahead of time what the focus of each of these units would be. With assessment-based units, teachers at the same grade level might very well be teaching different units of study. Because these units would focus on skills or strategies (rather than genres), kids would not only choose their topics during these units of study but also choose the genres, thus giving them more practice with familiar genres.

One concern teachers voiced about this approach was that some kids would become overwhelmed with making decisions and would either write genreless pieces or be unsure what genre to choose. We decided that we could solve that by generating a chart at the start of these units about the genres or forms that the kids had either learned or seen in the world. Kindergarten kids, for example, might not have been taught a whole lot of genres, but they certainly could notice signs, lists, cards, and different kinds of books they had seen in the world and give their best shot at writing one.

Let's see how this conversation changed the kindergarten curriculum calendar (refer back to Figure 6.1). The teachers began the year by launching the writing workshop. For this unit we purposely didn't specify a genre because we wanted to give kids paper, pencils, and markers and see what types of books they would make on their own. Once they were in the midst of making books, we could then give names to them:

- Wow, so it looks like you're writing a story about something that happened to you, like some of the books I read to you during read-aloud.
- It seems like you are making a book that teaches people all about the park—a nonfiction book.
- It seems like you are making a book that tells people about how fun your dad is.

During this time kids got to play around with writing different types of books and then began to realize that there is more than one type of book in the world. In December we planned for an assessment-based unit, when the kids could practice writing in the different forms and genres that they had learned and tried up until then. Then we planned another assessment-based unit for March so that once again the kindergarten children would have a chance to choose the genres they'd write in. After we decided when to have assessment units, we brainstormed what those units might be. While we did think it would be helpful to have a short list of possible assessment units, by no means was it exhaustive. We knew that when we assessed kids before the units, other unit ideas would come up. The teachers came up with an initial list based on the types of skills and strategies their kids had needed in the past (see Figure 6.2).

These assessment-based units would foster self-directed learners in some distinct ways. First, the practice would increase their confidence. It would also help them find and nurture their passion for particular genres. A child who loves poetry is bound to write poems during an assessment-based unit and a child who loves informational writing is bound to write some sort of informational text during this time. Finally, because children would be choosing the genres, they would need to self-regulate their learning; they'd need to remember and reflect upon what they had learned and then make decisions about what genres they wanted to try again.

FIGURE 6.2 IDEAS FOR KINDERGARTEN ASSESSMENT-BASED UNITS

Possible Assessment-Based Units

- Illustration Study for Storybooks (setting, characters, showing change)
- Illustration Study for Informational Books (close-ups, captions, diagrams)
- Stretching Words and Listening to Beginning, Middle, and End Sounds
- Using Words You Know (sight word study)
- Rereading Writing
- Effective Leads
- Effective Endings

Plan for a Year That Applies Kids' Recent and Prior Learning

We also wanted to create a curriculum calendar that deliberately pushed kids to use what they had learned either during previous units of study or during previous years. Doing this would get kids into the habit of trusting themselves first rather than always relying upon others. It would also help them see how much they knew, thus raising their confidence. We decided we could do this by planning for a quick publish and assessment at the start of the year. For most grades, this quick publish and assessment would take place over one to three days. Kids would be asked to write in the three text types that appear in the Common Core State Standards: narrative, expository, and argument/opinion. We knew that during this quick publish we could not and should not help kids, but rather we should use this time to see what they already knew so that we could plan each of the individual units accordingly.

We decided to plan for an abbreviated version of this in kindergarten since this was the kids' first experience in school. Specifically, we planned for a one-day assessment during which we would give them paper, pencils, and markers and let them know that they could draw and/or write about anything they wanted, and if they wanted to make it into a book like ones they had seen in the world, they could. Then we could plan for a year that would build upon what we would discover through this assessment.

Plan for a Year That Connects Reading and Writing

We also thought that we could plan for a year of self-directed learning by trying to connect the reading and writing curriculum calendars. If kids are learning about similar concepts at the same time in both reading and writing, they are bound to get more of an in-depth understanding. An added benefit to planning this way is that it makes your teaching more efficient and more effective.

The kindergarten team at PS 230 planned for some reading-writing connections. In reading they planned for an emergent reading unit of study during the month of October. During this study kids would be approximating reading. They would be listening to their teacher read rich storybooks and then later reading those books themselves, both reading the pictures and remembering the words of the story. Because this study would take place in October, the teachers planned to have an illustration study in writing in October and a true story unit in November. Reading the illustrations during the emergent reading unit of study would certainly help them draw illustrations during the illustration writing unit of study. Hearing and practicing the rich language of story in reading would assist them when trying to tell and write true stories in the writing unit in November. In December they planned to do early print strategies in reading and follow up on these print strategies in a unit of study on writing for many purposes. During this unit of study the teachers planned to show kids how to listen for sounds and record letters in different types of writing. In January they planned for a nonfiction reading unit of study followed by a nonfiction writing unit of study in February.

● The Fifth-Grade Curriculum Planning Meeting

Let's look at the same strategies when planning a fifth-grade curriculum. We'll once again pay attention to how planning in this manner nurtures students to become more self-directed. In Figure 6.3 you can see the grade 5 curriculum calendar.

Plan for a Year That Teaches New Genres and *Gives Kids Plenty of Practice in Them*

In the upper grades the idea of giving kids lots of practice in the genres they would learn was a bit more challenging to plan for than it was in the primary grades because as part of the upper-grade process, kids typically use their writer's notebooks to plan and prepare. Then they use that thinking and planning to come out of their notebooks to draft, revise, edit, and publish one single piece of writing for each unit.

In order for the upper-grade kids to get more practice within one genre study, we decided that in every unit of study they would go through the entire writing process twice—once as part of the unit of study and then a second time either for

FIGURE 6.3 GRADE 5 CURRICULUM CALENDAR

Grade 5
September: Quick Publish and Launching the Writing Workshop/Memoir October–November: Personal Essay December: Feature Article January: Research-Based Argument February: Literary Essay March–April: Test Prep (comparative essay) April–May: Assessment-Based Unit June: Writing in the Content Areas: Informational Piece (format to be determined)

homework or during any extra time they had during writing workshop. In the past kids were freewriting for homework and during any extra time they had during writing workshop. Although freewriting can have a powerful effect on kids, the teachers found that often the freewriting did not connect to the units of study. That meant they were not getting additional practice in the genres they were studying. Often, kids struggled with what to write, so they just filled up the page with anything, without giving it much thought. The teachers liked the idea of having kids publish more than once during a unit of study because this meant they got to practice the genre again. It also had the potential to lift the level of both their homework and their independent work in writing workshop. Furthermore, by working through the genre with less scaffolding, kids would need to self-regulate their learning. Specifically, they would need to create goals for themselves during this process so that they could go from idea to finished piece in a timely manner.

During the fifth-grade planning meeting we found some key places in the year where we felt we could ask kids to publish a second time. One place we thought this would work especially well was during the argument essay unit of study. During this unit, each student was going to publish an argument essay related to the social studies content. The student would choose an idea within this content that he or she felt strongly about. We agreed that each kid could fairly easily publish a second piece on a topic of his or her choice. The kids already had some experience with persuasive writing in third and fourth grades. Therefore, we thought it would be easier for them to do this work independently. We understood that the pieces might not be as strong as the ones that we were teaching into (we would never tell the kids this), but we knew that the additional practice would get kids to become more self-directed. We also felt that kids could publish twice during the literary essay unit of study.

To ensure kids had additional practice, we identified some places in the year where we could add some assessment-based studies. We decided to plan for one right after the launching unit of study and one right after the testing unit of study in April. The teachers also did what the kindergarten teachers did: they created a short, incomplete list of possible assessment-based units, knowing that many more ideas would come up as they assessed their students in preparation for these units (see Figure 6.4).

Plan for a Year That Applies Kids' Recent and Prior Learning

The fifth-grade team decided to start the year with a three-day quick publish where kids would write a piece in each of the three text types found in the Common Core State Standards (narrative, expository, and opinion/argument) without teacher

FIGURE 6.4 IDEAS FOR GRADE 5 ASSESSMENT-BASED UNITS

Possible Assessment-Based Units

- Sentence Study
- Transitional Words to Use in Expository Texts
- Transitional Words to Use in Narrative Texts
- Organization: Using Your Notebook to Organize and Drafting with Organization in Mind

intervention. Talking about the quick publish led us to an interesting conversation. We wondered whether these types of quickly published pieces and assessments would truly show us what kids knew. Put yourself in your kids' shoes for a moment. Imagine having learned a type of writing the year before. You've now had a summer break and have not written in this genre for quite a while. Also imagine that you have a new teacher who may word things in a slightly different way than the teacher you had the year before. Imagine that teacher asks you to write in this genre. Then, imagine being assessed on that writing. You might know significantly more than what the assessment reveals. One teacher worried that the assessment would not truly show us how much kids knew, which would lead to teaching kids in a less rigorous way. We wondered how we could rectify this.

In Chapter 3, I spoke about how the teachers in South Street School worked hard on having some consistent charts and then moving those charts to the next grade the following year. We wondered if we could get a more authentic assessment if we gathered relevant charts from the previous year and had those charts up in the room during the assessment. We would not and should not teach into these charts. Rather, we would just point to them (or perhaps read them out loud) during the assessment as concrete and visual reminders of what the students had learned the year before. You'll hear more about this idea in the next chapter.

By having those assessments early, as well as incorporating assessment-based units throughout the year, the teachers would essentially be saying to their kids that they believed and trusted that the kids already knew something about these genres. Also, by starting this so early in the year, they would be setting a precedent that they'd expect kids to use what they knew in every unit of study.

Plan for a Year That Connects Reading and Writing

There were a few ways that the grade 5 teachers planned to connect their reading and writing curriculum calendars. First, they purposely staggered their nonfiction reading unit of study (October) with their feature article study in writing (November). Both of these studies focused on expository texts and the structures within. The plan was to provide kids with comprehension instruction in reading expository text structures in October and then reinforce and elevate the instruction by having them write in those same structures in November. In October they would have a chance to learn new information so that when they wrote feature articles, kids could have the option to write about the topics from their reading unit of study.

Another way they planned to connect reading and writing was to teach a personal essay study in October and November, when the kids would explore a big idea about themselves or a person they knew. In December they planned a unit of study in reading that focused on characters and what they learned about these characters by following them across a text. Often when we think about reading-writing connections, we think about how the reading work can support and enhance the writing work. As a result, we usually put the reading work before or at the same time as the writing work. In this instance, they planned for the writing work to come a month before the reading work. There is research to suggest that composing something first can actually support comprehension. It certainly makes sense. When a student writes in a particular genre, it is bound to help her when reading in that same genre since she's already examined it closely as a writer. In this instance, each kid would be studying a character (either the students or a person he or she knew), discovering a big idea about this character, and then exploring that idea in an essay format. This kind of work was bound to help the kids a month later when they would explore the characters in the texts, try to come up with big ideas about these characters, and support these ideas with evidence from the text.

● Plan for Success

Having a well-planned curriculum is certainly helpful for creating a successful writing workshop. At PS 230, the teachers and I had great fun trying to figure out ways to plan the curriculum in a way that would nurture self-directed learners. We found that when you connect curriculum with self-directed learning, it can lead to a rigorous and engaging writing workshop. What could be better than that?

"Too often we ask children to arrive without having traveled."

—TOM ROMANO, EDUCATOR AND AUTHOR

CHAPTER 7

PLANNING UNITS OF STUDY THAT CREATE SELF-DIRECTED LEARNERS

In Chapter 6, I discussed how to deliberately plan a yearlong curriculum calendar that addresses both content and self-directed learning. In this chapter, you'll discover how to plan individual units of study while keeping both of those ideas in the forefront. First I define the different elements of unit planning. Then I discuss how each element, if planned carefully, can support your goal of creating self-directed learners.

Planning units of study in this manner will open up opportunities for your kids to become engaged, excited, persistent, resourceful self-starters who go over and beyond what you teach in your focus lessons, conferences, and shares. It will also open opportunities for you to become more self-directed as well. Specifically, you will see how planning in this particular way is not always easy but enables you to own and understand the unit rather than just implement it. You'll become more resilient when there are bumps in the road and more of a self-starter as you watch your kids and plan teaching around what you discover while watching them.

The Key Elements to Planning a Genre Unit of Study

Following are the essential parts you'll want to consider while planning genre studies in your classroom:
- backward planning
- preassessment
- immersion

- planning and preparing in the writer's notebook (for grades 3–5)
- the bulk of the study: planning focus lessons for drafting, revising, and editing
- anticipated problems
- physical environment
- publishing
- formative and summative assessment
- reflection

As I explained earlier both in Chapter 1 and in Chapter 6, there are some units of study that are focused on skills and strategies rather than genres. When planning those units of study you'll notice that some but not all of these elements will apply. For more extensive information on each of these parts, as well as planning non-genre units of study, I encourage you to read Matt Glover and Mary Alice Berry's book *Projecting Possibilities for Writing: The How, What and Why of Designing Units of Study* (2012). At the end of this book, you'll find some templates to help you plan your units of study (see Appendix).

Backward Planning

When talking about unit planning, Wiggins and McTighe (2005) emphasize the importance of backward design. I couldn't agree more. Essentially, this means you begin planning a unit of study with what you hope you will achieve by the end of the study. When you know where you want to go, it is much easier to get there. Here are a few questions you'll want to consider right at the start of a unit of study:
- What is the specific genre I am studying with my kids?
- What will students' final products look like?
- Who will be the readers (audience) for my students' writing? Or will the students decide who their readers (their audience) will be?
- Will these readers read the piece throughout the unit of study or only at the end?
- What is the exact date that I will expect students to be ready to publish and celebrate?
- What are my goals or objectives for the unit of study?

It will also help you more fully understand the unit if you write a piece in that genre.

There are a few important ways that the decisions you make during this early stage of unit planning will help your students become more self-directed. First, consider how knowing your audience makes you more self-directed. Knowing their audience from the beginning gets kids to be more engaged and more persistent in creating published pieces that communicate their ideas clearly. In my earlier days of teaching I made the mistake of not having kids consider audience until the end of the study. They didn't have the chance to consider their audience throughout the unit. As part of the planning work in their writer's notebooks, many upper-grade kids make a decision about audience.

Deadlines and celebrations are other ways to keep students self-directed. They will keep students more engaged and excited throughout the study. It's easy to choose a deadline but not always as easy to stick to it. However, kids respond well to deadlines, especially the kids who work slowly or don't usually finish on time. The deadline will put a little skip in their steps; some outside pressure to finish in a reasonable amount of time is good for them in school as well as in life. There will always be something more to teach, which is why teachers often don't keep to deadlines, but your students will be better off if you end the unit and teach those skills and concepts in future units of study.

Don't forget to plan a celebration at the end of a unit of study. Years ago when I was taking a summer institute at the Teachers College Reading and Writing Project, my instructor said something that stayed with me. She said, "It's not always fun to write, but it's fun to have written." I spend hours each week writing. It is often grueling, exhausting, and just plain hard. What makes all the hard work worth it are the celebrations I have with my friends and colleagues at the end. Both my readers and the upcoming celebration are what keep me going on those hard writing days. If I need that to keep going, then our students need it as well. Often a writing celebration is an afterthought or an extra activity if there is time. It should be an essential part of every unit of study at every grade level. Celebrations shouldn't be time-consuming for you. They can be as simple as having a cup of juice and a few crackers with a buddy. Choose a simple celebration at the end of every unit of study over a more complicated one for only a few. Let kids know from the start about the celebration so they can look forward to it throughout the study.

When planning goals at the start of the unit, you may very well want to have some goals that are directly connected to self-directed learning. A good way to come up with these types of goals is to take a portion of a writing workshop to simply watch your kids and notice how they are or are not self-directed. Then, create goals based on what you notice. Here are some goals that a group of teachers from PS 24 in Brooklyn, New York made for their persuasive essay unit of study:

- At the end of this unit kids will know multiple ways to build their arguments.
- At the end of this unit kids will understand how to choose and use graphic organizers to gather research and plan their drafts.
- At the end of this unit kids will be able to use charts and mentor texts independently as vehicles to solve problems.

As you can see, the first goal was related to the genre, but the last two goals were related to nurturing kids to become more self-directed. Figure 7.1 is an assessment for observing your students and their abilities to be self-directed. Knowing what they can or cannot do in this area may help you decide on goals for self-directed learning.

Studying and writing in the genre that you are about to teach is important. It will help you become a more self-directed teacher. It will also help you become more confident, more engaged, and more of a self-starter. When things go wrong during the unit (and they will), you will be more resilient and more persistent in solving the issues because you'll have an in-depth understanding of the genre. The experience of studying and writing texts will also help you establish appropriate goals and objectives for the unit. With that being said, I know how busy teachers are and trying to write on top of a busy teacher's life is challenging. Here are some suggestions on how to bring some writing into your busy schedule without getting overwhelmed:

- Start slowly. Commit to trying it with one unit of study.
- Start slowly. Commit to writing in a specific genre for a short period of time, such as ten to fifteen minutes.
- Study and write in the genre as part of your unit planning with colleagues.
- Ask your principal if teachers can do some writing during a staff meeting as part of unit planning.

Preassessment

Assessing your students before the unit begins can help you plan the study so it will match your kids' strengths and needs. However, you want to be careful that you don't assess so much and so often that it overtakes your teaching. If you assess everything every day, it doesn't leave time for you to teach into what you discover.

FIGURE 7.1

● Unit of Study Assessment

Independent first, interdependent second: Are kids trying things on their own, or are they turning too quickly to others for help?

Confident: Do students feel good about their work? How do you know that?

Willing to take risks: Do kids try new things that might be hard or scary for them?

Excited: Is there a project-like feeling in your classroom?

Engaged: Are kids able to work for extended periods of time?

Persistent: Do your students work hard to solve their own problems or do they give up too easily?

Resilient: How do kids react when things don't go as planned?

Resourceful:

Are kids using charts to solve problems?

Are kids using mentor texts independently?

Are kids using the writing materials appropriately?

Self-starting: Are kids trying out things during writing workshop that are different and go beyond what you taught in focus lessons, conferences, and shares?

Self-regulating: Do kids create their own goals and work toward those goals?

With this in mind, one option for how to start a genre writing unit of study is with a preassessment. It's not necessary to start every unit of study this way, especially if you do a quick publish and assessment at the start of the year. If you begin the year with a quick publish, look at those samples to help you understand what students already know or don't know about a specific genre.

If you do decide to assess your kids at this point, remember that you shouldn't be helping them but rather watching what they do without you. Once students finish this assessment, you'll take a look at the writing samples to revise and tweak your unit goals.

There are many benefits to assessment but one is that kids are asked to show what they know without enlisting the help of others. This activity certainly helps kids become more self-directed.

To illustrate the power of preassessment, I want to share the work that Kristin Merkle did with her first-grade students. Kristen was about to begin an informational book unit of study. She consulted with the kindergarten teachers at her school and discovered that while each teacher taught the unit slightly differently, the entire team taught the following three ideas:

1. Informational books teach their readers more than one thing.
2. Informational writers help teach readers by labeling parts of their pictures.
3. Informational books have pictures that teach.

Kristen wanted to display (but not teach from) the informational charts that the kindergarten teachers had used. Her hope was that the kids could use those charts to remind them of all that they already knew. Unfortunately, the kindergarten teachers had not kept their charts, so Kristen created her own chart with the three ideas. Kristen began the preassessment by pointing to and reading the chart. She didn't reteach anything. She just reminded them that they had learned these ideas last year and that they could use the ideas to each make an informational book. When kids said they were unsure about what to do, Kristen told them not to worry but to do the best they could. She thought that once they got started, they would begin to remember some things about informational books.

Sure enough, they did! Figure 7.2 contains three writing samples that came from Kristen's preassessment. These pieces span the range of the class and reveal quite a bit of understanding about informational books. All of the kids understood that

FIGURE 7.2 WRITING SAMPLES FROM INFORMATIONAL BOOK PREASSESSMENT

All Abut Cars

I know that cars have enjins. They have gas.

1

Cars have seest. They have weels. They have horns.

2

Cars have windows. Cars can be fast. Some cars have

3

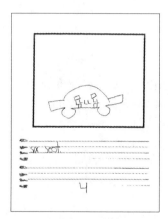

six seet.

4

All About Tiger's

Tigers are donjres they eat peoplps and animals.

1

Tigers have strip's all over it boty.

2

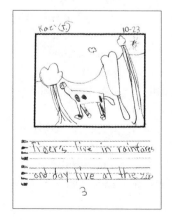

Tiger's live in rainfores and day live at the zoo

3

Tigers are big cars they are biger then animals.

4

If it niete time the tigers get yellow

informational books teach and they all included more than one fact. There was some evidence of pictures that taught and even some labeling within the pictures. This preassessment led Kristen to lift the level of her goals. Kristen also felt that the assessment activity built up her kids' confidence. They were able to see how much they already knew.

Here's one possible protocol when assessing student writing during the preassessment:

- **Description:** What do you notice on the page? Describe the writing simply and plainly.
- **Questions:** What do you want to ask students based on what you notice?
- **Interpretation:** What are some similar things these students seem to be working on? What patterns do you see across these writing pieces?
- **Classroom implications:** What does this mean for setting goals for the upcoming unit of study?

Immersion

No matter what the genre, no matter how busy the year, it's essential that once you've conducted a preassessment, you plan for multiple days of immersion (three to five days). Immersion is a period of time when kids are studying the genre. They can do this by studying texts like the ones they are about to write. You can also support immersion by conducting a write-aloud, as I described in Chapter 5. The hope is that all of this work will help kids feel more confident and ready to write independently in this genre.

You might be uncomfortable with the idea of students not writing during the immersion phase of a unit of study. Don't be! In my travels as a literacy consultant, I've discovered that the quality of writing in classrooms that start with an extended immersion phase is much higher than that in classrooms that do only a quick immersion or none at all. While it's true that the kids aren't doing much writing that first week, they are doing two things that will drastically improve their writing: studying the genre and writing collaboratively with their class. I would also suggest that during this first week you make sure that students are doing plenty of writing in other parts of the day (writing responses to reading, explaining how they solved a math problem, writing what they learned in social studies, etc.). During the week of immersion, upper-grade students may even be jotting down writing ideas in their writer's notebooks.

SAMPLE SCHEDULE FOR WRITING WORKSHOP DURING THE IMMERSION PHASE OF A UNIT OF STUDY

1. Teacher conducts a focus lesson on how to notice craft techniques in the writing.
2. Students work in pairs and teacher confers.
3. Class comes together to share.
4. Class composes a write-aloud.

Many well-intentioned teachers view immersion solely as a time to expose kids to the goals of the upcoming unit of study. For example, if the writing unit of study were realistic fiction and one of the lessons in the unit were about dialogue, the teacher might use one of the immersion sessions to put up some examples of dialogue. Once she put up some examples of dialogue, she might point out a few things about the dialogue (e.g., the punctuation used or dialogue tags). Another goal might be great beginnings, so on a different day she might put up a few examples of great beginnings as way to prepare the kids for what she would teach next. Although exposing kids to the goals of the study is certainly a part of immersion, it's not the only or most important part. If we want kids to become more self-directed, then we must use immersion as a vehicle to get kids to discover independently all sorts of things about the genre, not just the unit goals. You want your immersion to have a spirit of inquiry or discovery to it.

Immersion should also not occur just as a whole-group activity. If you want kids to discover a lot, then it must happen in partnerships as well.

It's important to accept and revel in everything they notice. Whether they are noticing the pictures, the words, one of your goals, or something that seems completely obscure, remember that the more they notice, the more they can try in their own writing without your help. This type of noticing will help your kids to become self-starters. They'll be filled to the brim not only with what you have taught in your focus lessons and conferences but also with what they discovered about the genre.

Throughout immersion, you'll also want to remind kids that the purpose of studying these texts is to get ideas for their own drafts or books. I often sound like a broken record during immersion because I am constantly reminding kids that they will be writing soon and all of this should be giving them cool ideas. During immersion, I remind kids over and over again they can try anything they notice even if I don't teach that concept later in the unit. If you don't remind them of the purpose of immersion, they may enjoy it but not apply anything they notice to their future drafts or books. With older kids, I may give them sticky notes to jot down their ideas.

During immersion, you'll also want to conduct a write-aloud with your class. The write-aloud will serve as a scaffold for kids because they will have the opportunity to orally practice with the class what they will eventually be doing independently.

Planning and Preparing in the Writer's Notebook (Grades 3–5)

Once K–2 kids have gone through the immersion phase, most teachers will move them to drafting multiple pieces in their folders. In a grades 3–5 classroom, however, most teachers have kids think, plan, and prepare for their drafts in their writer's notebooks. Because second grade is a transitional year, some second-grade teachers might consider giving their kids a smaller version of a writer's notebook called a try-it pad. Inside of this try-it pad, the kids might try a few things before or while they are drafting as way to transition into longer and more in-depth planning in grade 3.

Next, I want to share a few tips for how to conduct this part of the unit for grades 3–5 students so that the writer's notebook helps improve drafts and gets them to become more self-directed. I begin by showing kids an example of a writer's notebook with evidence of planning, preparing, and thinking. Often, I share my own notebook, making sure to point out all of my planning.

You might be wondering if showing them so many notebook entries in one day might be overwhelming. Wouldn't you be better off showing them one entry a day across the week? While I understand the desire to share small sections of your writing, the problem is that it will make kids dependent upon you because they will have to wait to try each strategy. Most kids will try only the one strategy you showed them that day and won't know what to do once they're finished. By exposing them to many strategies on day one, you are setting them up to be more resourceful. When they think they are finished in their notebooks, they'll have more to do because they've already been exposed to many strategies on the first day. Once I give them the big picture on day one and show them many strategies, I then teach a few of them in depth.

The Bulk of the Study: Planning Focus Lessons for Drafting, Revising, and Editing

Continue to teach into your goals by having kids draft, revise, edit, and then each bring at least one piece to publication. Some teachers brainstorm long lists of things they could teach, usually more than is possible. Others devise a day-by-day sequence of what they might do. Both of these ways tend to be problematic. The first method is problematic because having a long list will make you feel scattered and not connected to your goals. A day-by-day sequence does not leave space for you to adjust to concerns that arise while teaching. For example, during your unit of study, you might do a focus lesson related to your goals and find that your students need more instruction than you anticipated. Or perhaps there is another teaching point that you initially thought would take a few days but now realize won't take much time because most of your kids understand it. Therefore, you want to move onto something else and gather the kids who need more instruction into a small group. Perhaps a concept pops out that you didn't intend to teach but kids clearly need to succeed in this genre.

Instead of either of those approaches, I suggest planning a smaller list of possible teaching ideas that go back to your intended goals. This way, all of your teaching will be aimed toward helping kids achieve the goals that you set out for them, as well as giving you some flexibility in what you teach and for how long.

In Chapter 8, I go into more depth about what your focus lessons during this time might look and sound like. If you do have a longer list of teaching ideas, I would divide that list into what you think you'll teach in your whole-class lessons and what you'll teach during conferences and small-group work.

I've discussed the importance of planning for what you might teach but being careful not to plan a day-to-day sequence so that you can assess throughout the unit and teach concepts according to what your kids show you they need or want. Organizing your teaching in this way helps students become more self-directed.

Anticipated Problems

It's helpful to talk with colleagues about potential problems that might arise during this unit as well as possible solutions. That way, you can trouble-shoot and solve anticipated problems before they even occur. In *Projecting Possibilities for Writers*, Matt Glover and Mary Alice Berry (2012) have some great questions to help you imagine some of the potential problems that might occur during the unit. Here are just a few:

- Think about the things that challenged your students the last time you taught this unit. What aspect of this unit seemed to be the easiest and the most difficult for previous students?
- Consider issues that are typical for students at your grade level. What do most second or fourth graders do? What is developmentally appropriate for the students you work with?
- Consider areas where you will need more data about students before you can make an informed decision. (98)

Just as we want kids to understand that there will be bumps in the road as they write, we need to understand that there will be bumps in the road while we teach. These bumps don't necessarily mean that our teaching is off. Often, they just mean that we have to work on some trouble spots.

It can be helpful to talk to colleagues about some of the bumps that occur during the unit and get suggestions on how you might solve them. Likewise, it can be helpful to take notes on problems you anticipate encountering and list some possible solutions.

Physical Environment

Another essential part of unit planning is to consider your classroom environment. There are several types of charts you'll want. First you'll want brainstorm charts. During immersion, kids will notice many things about the genre. Of course, you wouldn't want to teach all of those things in one unit. It's helpful to chart what kids notice so that they can refer to it throughout the unit. You'll also want charts that outline your goals for the unit along with writing samples (published and kids') for each of these goals. You'll also want to create charts that introduce new language or vocabulary. For example, if you're in an informational book unit of study, you will want to teach and then chart language such as *all*, *most*, and *some* since those words will help link information in a more literary way. If you're in a persuasive essay unit of study, you might want to teach and then chart language such as *for example* and *another reason some people might think*. Finally, you'll want to ensure that mentor texts are an integral part of your classroom environment.

You'll want to plan for how you will teach and then display both charts and mentor texts in a way that will encourage kids to use them on their own. One way to move kids toward using the materials in the classroom independently is to include mentor texts that relate to the goals. For example, if you have been teaching kids about including specific examples to back up ideas in their informational texts, then you might want to have a small labeled crate of mentor texts that are examples of this. You will also want to include in your unit plan lessons that model for kids how to use these mentor texts and charts to solve the inevitable problems that will arise for them during the unit of study.

Publishing

Publishing is the time when your students will fancy up their writing so that it will be appealing to their readers. There are many ways to do this. It can be as simple as making a cover page for the piece or coloring in the pictures that accompany the writing. Students could type or copy over their pieces. Proceed with both of those options cautiously. Many schools have not caught up to the world of technology, so if kids do type their pieces, it can become tedious for a number of reasons. Kids may not have the typing skills to type quickly or there may not be enough computers to enable your class to finish in a timely manner. Copying over can be very tedious for students as well. Many students may try to make their drafts shorter if they know they will be asked to copy them over during publishing. Ultimately, I make the decision on whether or not to have kids copy over their pieces of writing by asking myself if the amount of time it will take them is worth what they will learn.

Teachers also ask me whether a published piece should be 100 percent correct. I believe that in the younger grades, their final pieces will have some words spelled correctly and some spelled incorrectly. It reveals young kids' attempts to use what they know to figure out words. For example, if a first-grade child writes about going ice-skating, I don't think it particularly matters whether he spells *ice-skating* correctly; however, I do want him to spell sight words such as *was*, *they*, and *went* correctly. As kids get older and they acquire more skills, my expectations of what they do while editing and publishing become greater. However, I still think it's unreasonable to expect a perfectly edited piece of writing.

Some teachers visit each student, correcting the child's piece with him or her. I don't think this is a wise idea. It takes a long time and kids can't possibly internalize all the corrections you make. If you feel strongly that published means 100 percent correct, I recommend that you collect writing pieces after kids have done their own editing work and correct the errors without the students present, very much the same way my copyeditors work.

When I visited Paula Jensvold's classroom she was about to publish. When I heard she was ending her unit, I was disappointed because I thought there wouldn't be much teaching for me to observe at this point in the process. What I found instead was incredible teaching! Paula was showing her kids how to use mentor texts to create beautiful covers for their personal narratives. Watching her reminded me of the missed opportunity many of us have when we don't carefully plan for the publishing phase of a unit of study. Here's how Paula's teaching unfolded over three days and how she used publishing to get kids to become more resourceful and more independent:

On the first day, she used a few mentor texts to look at covers. During the lessons, she asked the kids, "What do you notice that you could use when you make your own cover?" The next day, she made an anchor chart titled "Time to Publish!

What Do We Do?" She asked the kids to help her create this chart. The children listed several things: add a cover, add a title, add color to pictures, reread, fix up words, check word wall words, add detail, make sure the pictures match the words, and use lots of colors. The children then set their own individual goals for the day on how they would publish.

On the third day, she asked, "What can you do today to continue your publishing?" Children said they could use the chart to get an idea. They could use a mentor text. During the share that day, one little girl shared how she had added a dedication page by using a mentor text all by herself. We added that idea to our original anchor chart. Another little girl shared that she added an about-the-author part after using a mentor text.

Assessment

You'll want to plan to create checklists and rubrics throughout the study. At times, teachers make these assessments more complicated than they need to be. Rubrics and checklists should be directly connected to the established goals in the unit. For example, the third-grade team at PS 230 came up with the following goals for its informational book unit of study:

- At the end of this unit, kids will understand how to organize their information into categories.
- At the end of this unit, kids will understand how to write facts that define.
- At the end of this unit, kids will understand how to write facts that describe.
- At the end of this unit, kids will understand how to include informational book language in their writing.

Once the teachers had these goals in mind, it was much easier to create different types of checklists. Here is a checklist they made to help students know when they were ready to draft:

YOU KNOW YOU'RE READY TO DRAFT WHEN:

- you have created a table of contents (or some other form of organizing system) that helps you know the categories for your draft and their order;
- you have decided upon the words that you'll define in your draft;
- you have checked some of the book language that you're hoping to include; and
- you have practiced describing your topic.

As you can see, the checklist is directly connected to the goals. They could have also easily created an assessment rubric that was connected to the goals of the unit. You'll also want to plan for an end-of-unit assessment to see how much the students have learned throughout the unit. If you did a preassessment, it would make sense to align the end-of-unit assessment with it, as that would make it easier to measure growth.

Creating rubrics and checklists that can be used throughout the study as well as at the end of the study will be helpful to both you and your students. They will help you understand your kids' strengths and needs. They will also help your students understand what their writing goals are and teach them how to self-regulate their work.

Reflection

Once your unit is complete, it's helpful to reflect. Think about what went well so that you can integrate those parts into future units and about what didn't work so that you can tweak that part of the unit and make it more successful in the future.

Teacher reflection is an important part of unit planning. Doing this will boost your confidence because as you reflect, you'll learn more and more about how to plan the study in a way that will support all learners.

Take the Challenge

Planning a unit of study in writing is an endlessly exciting but challenging endeavor. Hopefully as you plan and implement units of study (using the templates in the Appendix), both you and your students will feel empowered, confident, and energized. What could be more important than that?

> "The best teacher is the one who suggests rather than dogmatizes, and inspires his listener with the wish to teach himself."
>
> —EDWARD BULWER-LYTTON, AUTHOR

CHAPTER 8

DESIGNING FOCUS LESSONS, CONFERENCES, AND SHARES FOR SELF-DIRECTED LEARNING

As I walked into Trudy Cioffi's third-grade classroom, I couldn't help but notice how happy, engaged, and excited her kids were. The students were too busy taking care of morning routines to even notice me. After a few minutes, Trudy handed me a pile of beautiful pictures and told me they were the designs that her kids had created for the upcoming T-shirt contest. As I glanced through the pile, it was clear that every design was different, well thought out, and filled with personality.

After a few minutes, a parent came in to talk to the class about the T-shirt contest. The kids listened intently and asked him many questions. Watching this encounter made me even more excited to work with Trudy and her class. I couldn't wait to try to nurture the type of self-directed behavior I was already seeing with the T-shirt contest.

Common sense tells us that the purpose of having a writing workshop is to teach kids how to improve their writing. Of course, this is true, but at the same time you want your instruction to create self-directed learners.

▊ Focus Lessons That Help Kids Become More Self-Directed

Focus lessons are a time when you gather your entire class and teach the group something. You can purposefully structure focus lessons so that kids become more self-directed.

End Your Focus Lessons with Uncertainty

Make the ends of your lessons open-ended. This sounds a bit strange, I'm sure. We are so used to thinking that the ends of lessons should provide closure for kids, that a tip such as ending with uncertainty sounds counterproductive. After all, closure is neat and tidy and uncertainty is messy. But messiness in your teaching allows you to linger longer with a concept, get your students' input, and assess their understanding of what you've taught. Plus the reality is that most things are not neat and tidy, and we confuse kids even more when we pretend that they are. Peter Johnston (2012) speaks about the idea of creating a classroom where all children become more comfortable with uncertainty. He says, "We can change children's comfort with uncertainty by changing the conversational structures that fill their lives, or by changing the situation" (63).

● A Focus Lesson

On the day I visited, Trudy decided to do a focus lesson on the connection between a writer's notebook, booklets, and draft paper (Trudy had her students draft both in booklets and on loose-leaf paper). We decided on this lesson because Trudy had noticed that many of her kids were using their notebooks to draft rather than as a place to plan and prepare their drafts. She ended her focus lesson that day by saying, "So, children, today you can decide whether or not you want to continue in your writer's notebook to plan or take a booklet or loose-leaf paper to start drafting." Although this focus lesson was tidy, it had the potential to shut down dialogue and cause students to become dependent upon the teacher. Children would probably assume that what Trudy said in the lesson would always be correct and believe that there would never be a reason to draft in their notebooks. But what you teach won't always work. On that very day, Matthew and Madi ended up drafting their ideas in their writer's notebooks. After speaking with them, we realized that it actually worked for them. There will always be a Matthew or a Madi in your classroom that "messes up" and breaks the rules of your neat, tidy lessons.

As Trudy and I spoke afterward, we tried to imagine how that same lesson might have sounded if she had taught the exact same material but included more uncertainty. She might have said something like this: "Today I talked to you about how the notebook is a place to plan and the booklets and loose-leaf paper are certainly places to draft your projects. I don't know if it will always work this way for every one of you in every writing piece. As you work together to produce your very best writing, let me know what you discover."

Another way to end this lesson with uncertainty rather than closure would be to simply say: "I just talked to you about ways to use a writer's notebook and booklets. Are there other ways you could do this?" Although the students' responses would make the focus lesson longer, it's definitely worth asking for their input on occasion. It's another way to create a classroom culture that believes that ideas and concepts grow as a group thinks, agrees, disagrees, and tries things together. By ending a focus lesson with uncertainty, you can encourage kids to become self-starters.

Linger Longer

One of the reasons that teachers yearn for closure in their focus lessons has to do with time constraints. Many teachers introduce a new concept in every focus lesson, so there simply is no time for messiness. The problem with teaching focus lessons in this manner is that some students can't learn the material in one day. Even if they could, their understanding would be superficial. There is a way to address this. You can linger longer with what you are teaching by having multiple days of focus lessons that delve into the same content.

When I first moved to Hoboken, New Jersey, I found that parking spaces were extremely small and parking in one of them was quite a feat, especially for someone like me who struggles with all things spatial. Many people tried to give me quick lessons. Even after those quick lessons, I still didn't feel secure. When I did try to park independently I caused serious damage to my car. It wasn't that I couldn't learn to park the car; I just needed to work harder at it. Finally, when my mom visited me, she worked with me on parking the car over a series of days rather than with just one quick lesson. Only after she lingered with the concept did I feel comfortable enough to give parking independently a try.

My parking experience is exactly why I don't ask kids to try something new after just one focus lesson. Instead I linger longer with a teaching point and have kids make decisions about exactly when they will try out what I've taught. Organizing your lessons this way is more likely to increase your students' self-directedness because it gives students the time to build their confidence with the material. It will also encourage them to be self-starters, because although they will have to try what you taught at some point, they will decide exactly when.

If you were to teach Trudy's lesson for only one day, you might feel pressured to say something like, "Today it is your job to use your notebook as a planning tool or today it is your job to draft using a booklet or loose-leaf paper." Again, the problem with this wording is that if they don't understand the concept (which many won't after only one focus lesson) they will come straight to you for help. Many students will also worry that they will be unable to independently implement what you taught that day. Although Trudy did plan to teach the relationship between writer's notebooks and drafts over time, she didn't explicitly share this. She realized that in the future she needed to include language in her focus lessons that would help kids understand that she would be teaching a concept over time and it would be up to them to decide exactly when to try it. Of course there are always some kids who will need some nudging. I watch out for those kids closely over multiple days of instruction and give them a quiet nudge if necessary.

Now that I have talked about *why* you should linger longer, I want to share *how* you might linger longer:

- Use a mentor text as an example of what you're teaching.
- Model by writing in front of your students and saying out loud what you're thinking as you write.
- Have your kids help you write a whole-class piece.
- Show them a writing sample from a child who has tried it.

A quick note about these different methods: In my early days of teaching I loved trying these different approaches. I would fill my plan book with a different method for each day of the week. If you do this, keep in mind that this plan is only a draft and should be revised as you watch your kids work with the content. For the most part you don't want to teach the same idea over and over again; you should tweak the concept based on what you notice while watching your kids work. You might notice that something confuses them and use subsequent lessons to untangle the confusions. Or perhaps you think that they have a surface understanding of a concept but as you watch and confer with them, you realize they are ready for a more in-depth understanding of this concept. Use the methods outlined above to deepen their understanding of the original content being taught.

End with Options

In *The Nuts and Bolts of Teaching Writing*, Lucy Calkins (2003) has created a wonderful structure for conducting focus lessons. She states that every focus lesson should include a connection, a teaching point, an active engagement, and a link (49–59). One purpose of a link at the end of a focus lesson is to generalize the lesson so kids understand how to integrate what they learned that day into their writing. I believe it's also important for the link to remind kids of all the options available during writing workshop.

In Trudy's lesson on writer's notebooks, booklets, and paper, the kids made the need for options crystal clear. When Trudy started talking about booklets and loose-leaf paper for drafting, Ella squirmed with excitement, remembering how much she loved booklets the year before. Rayden, on the other hand, let out a sigh of disappointment. He thought that Trudy was saying that everyone had to draft in a booklet. Trudy capitalized on this interaction. She let them know that they had the option to continue using their writer's notebooks to plan and think or move to booklets or loose-leaf paper to draft.

Trudy ended her lesson like this: "So, today and every day while writing, it's important to think about whether you need to draft or do more planning. Today, once you decide which one makes more sense, go ahead and do that. If you finish, you'll have to decide how to use the rest of your writing time. Certainly you can look at some of the charts that we've made this year that help you remember all the things you can do during writing workshop." Trudy pointed to particular charts and then let the kids go work.

Trudy linked the new content with their independent work, but she also high-lighted the other options they had during this time. This helps her kids be more independent and more resourceful.

End with Goal Setting

After you have taught the new material and kids understand what options they have that day, they should make a plan, set some goals, or do both. I might say: "Now it's time to start writing, so I want you to make some goals for your time today. Take a moment to think and let the person next to you know what you plan on doing first and then what you plan on doing next if and when you complete your first task." When I find that children are not taking this goal-making time seriously enough, I have them say their plans out loud to the entire group so I can get a status-of-the-class report. Some teachers have kids fill out goal sheets; you can see an example of one in Figure 8.1.

FIGURE 8.1 GOAL SHEET

Name: _____

Author's Goal Setting Sheet

Date	Today's goal . . .	What did I do today?
	○ Plan in my notebook ○ Draft ○ Re-read my writing ○ Add to or change my writing (revise) ○ Fix my writing (edit) ○ Other _____	Today I _____
	○ Plan in my notebook ○ Draft ○ Re-read my writing ○ Add to or change my writing (revise) ○ Fix my writing (edit) ○ Other _____	Today I _____
	○ Plan in my notebook ○ Draft ○ Re-read my writing ○ Add to or change my writing (revise) ○ Fix my writing (edit) ○ Other _____	Today I _____

Keep in mind that the purpose of a goal sheet is not to necessarily hold kids accountable to everything they said they would do. Children may or may not achieve what they set out to do that day. This is why it's important to not only make the goals but also go back, reflect, and revise the goals. Trudy created the goal sheet in Figure 8.1 to allow for this. Many teachers have kids reflect upon and revise their goals either as part of the share or at the end of the independent work time. Having children do this on a regular basis will help them self-regulate their learning.

Figure 8.2 includes sample language you can use in your lesson to encourage self-directed writing. You can use the questions in Figure 8.3 to assess how well your lessons support self-directed learning.

FIGURE 8.2 LANGUAGE ANGLED TOWARD SELF-DIRECTED LEARNERS

Say this . . .	Instead of this . . .
These are certainly things you can try in your own writing today and every day, but keep in mind you may very well discover other ways to describe your topic while working today. If you do, let us know during the share.	So today and every day while writing, it's important to describe your topic using color or shape words.
So today and whenever you are writing an informational piece of writing, one type of fact you can include is a fact that describes what your topic looks like. If it makes sense for you to do that today, I want you to try it. If it doesn't, put this lesson in your pocket and you'll try it over the next few days when it makes more sense.	So today you must add at least one fact that describes what your topic looks like.

FIGURE 8.3

● Focus Lesson Assessment

Did you end with some sort of uncertainty to keep the conversation going?
If not, how could you revise your lesson so that you would end with uncertainty?

What is your plan for teaching this concept over time? Did you make it clear to your
kids that they would have time to learn and try the new material? If you didn't, do you
think that one lesson was enough for kids to be self-directed with the material?

Did you remind children of all the other options they have during writing workshop?
If not, how could you revise the lesson so that they would be reminded of these options?

Did the kids do any sort of independent goal setting? If not, is there a way you
could have them plan and make goals (either orally or in writing) for the work they
hope to accomplish?

Did the kids reflect upon and revise their goals (if necessary)?
If not, when can they do this?

● Conferences That Help Kids Become More Self-Directed

Conferences, if done carefully, are yet another way to improve children's writing while at the same time helping them become more self-directed. Before we take a look at some of the conferences that Trudy and I had in her classroom, I want to share a simple management tip that will make a big difference in how self-directed kids are.

This suggestion might surprise you, but for the most part, I wouldn't have kids sign up for conferences. You should decide each day whom to confer with. It may seem as though a child is actually being self-directed by making a decision that he needs a conference. While that is true in some cases, I would argue that the ritual of signing up for a conference encourages kids to become dependent on the teacher. In essence, the children learn to solve a writing problem by signing up for a conference with the teacher. I want kids to view problems in writing as inevitable and know that the solution is not necessarily a conference with a teacher but their own hard work. I also want kids to understand that conferences are not just for solving problems; they can also occur when there seemingly are no problems. A conference can simply be a conversation with the teacher that can lead to new and surprising thoughts and ideas, as well as a renewed energy for a writing project.

COLLABORATION IN ACTION:
CONFERENCES

While Trudy and I conferred, we stopped, talked, and worked together to ensure that the conferences were angled toward teaching kids new content, as well as getting them to become more self-directed. You'll see the following ideas embedded in our conferences:

- Notice and name rather than simply praise.
- Make sure kids do as much work in the conference as you do (if not more). Make sure they understand that they did most of the work all by themselves.
- End a conference with goal setting.
- End a conference with uncertainty.

Conference 1

First, we had an unexpected conference with Mason because he seemed stuck. Rather than wait, Trudy felt like she should speak to him right away. He wanted to write a story about his brother. Trudy was careful to question him in a way that got him talking a lot. When she ended the conference, she asked him what his plan was for writing workshop that day. Surprisingly, Mason said he was going to write what Trudy had said. Whereas he thought Trudy did all the work, I thought he did the work. I extended the conference and helped Mason realize that these were his words, not his teacher's words.

Later on he caught my eye and let me know he was stuck again. I said I was confident that he would get himself unstuck and he did. When I questioned him later, he commented that, yes, he did get himself unstuck, but it was hard work. I pointed out how persistence paid off. In Figure 8.4 you can see Mason's writing and how much he actually got accomplished in one day of writing workshop even after he was convinced that he was stuck.

Conference 2

Next, we conferred with Matthew. Matthew was a student who seemed to prefer to linger longer in the notebook. He wrote about a fishing trip in his notebook and eagerly talked to us about his story, adding more details in his oral retelling and even more when he did a few quick sketches of the story in his notebook while

FIGURE 8.4 MASON'S WRITING

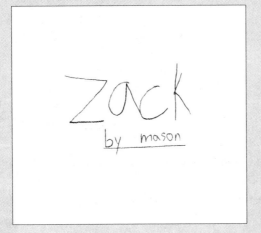

Zack
by mason

My brother is way older than me. He is in colej. Hee's in Florda. I was 1 when this hapend. My mom

gave me a stuffed animle called elmo and I beat it up. I tried to rip his head off but

I could not beacuase Zack toke it away and I cried so he gave it back to me. And

I riped elmo's head off. And I Laagfed.

talking with us. When we asked him about his plan for the day, he said it was to copy what he had written in his notebook into a booklet. Trudy and I looked at each other. We were both uncomfortable with him simply copying his words onto draft paper, but we knew that telling him that would defeat the purpose of making him more self-directed. He would then view conferences as a time when the teacher told you what to do rather than a time of collaboration.

I told Matthew that, when moving from planning to drafting, many writers try to change some of the original words. I asked him if he thought that making a deliberate effort to change or add some words was perhaps a good goal for him. I also pointed out all the additional details he shared during the conference. He thought about whether the goal made sense and agreed that it was a good goal. I told him that it might work for him or it might not, but I wanted him to try it and let us know what he discovered while trying it.

I want to point out a few things about this conference. Once Matthew committed to a goal, he had to try it. At the end of the conference, there was some goal setting. We also ended the conference with some uncertainty by asking him to let us know how it worked for him. He understood that it might work and it might not, which I believed would help him be more creative with the idea and pay more attention to it.

In Figure 8.5 you can see Matthew's writing in his notebook and the writing he did in his draft booklet.

Conference 3

Next, we conferred with Madi. Madi wrote a whole story in her writer's notebook and then told us during the conference that she had become overwhelmed when trying to copy the whole story into a draft booklet. Trudy was once again unsure about how to talk with her about this in a way that would teach her something new about writing while at the same time nurture her to become more self-directed. I asked Madi why she had decided to write the whole story in her notebook. She said that it helped her think of all the parts. That's when I realized that she might be using the notebook as a thinking tool. I then shared with her that it seemed as though she was using her notebook as a thinking tool and she agreed. I was purposely naming what I noticed rather than simply praising her on the great job she did using her notebook to think. Let's think about the difference between noticing and naming and being positive. For years, I told teachers to compliment or praise kids before teaching something new. Then I realized the problem with praising before you teach is that

FIGURE 8.5 MATTHEW'S WRITING

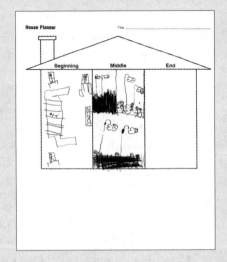

My Favorite Things
· army
· FAMILY
·
·
·

MAtt
weh I weht fishing.

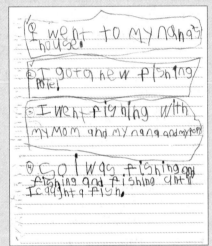

① I went to my nana's house.
② I got a new fishing pole.
③ I went fishing with my mom and my nana and my pop.
④ So I was fishing and fishing and fishing and I caught a fish.

kids will come to rely on your compliments or praise in order to continue doing quality work. On any given day when you neglect to compliment them, they might think that their work is no longer good. If you notice and name what children are doing, as I did in Madi's conference, it helps them rely on themselves and the work that they are doing. Doing this will get kids more excited, more engaged, and most importantly more confident about trying the work on their own.

I then extended Madi's strategy of thinking in her notebook by asking her if she thought it would make sense to use her notebook to consider which part of

FIGURE 8.5 MATTHEW'S WRITING, *CONT*.

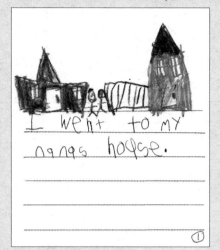

I went to my nanas house.
①

I got a new fishing pole!
②

I went fishing with my mom and my nana and my poppy.
③

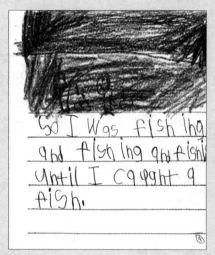

So I was fishing and fishing and fishing until I caught a fish.
④

the story was the important part and draft only that part. She felt like that would help. I reminded her that this would be a great strategy not only for today but in other situations as well. I once again ended with uncertainty by asking her to give us feedback on how this eventually worked for her. Figure 8.6 shows the work that Madi did both in her notebook and in her draft booklet.

Figure 8.7 includes sample language you can use in your conferences to encourage self-directed writing. You can use the questions in Figure 8.8 to assess how well your conferences support self-directed learning.

FIGURE 8.6 MADI'S WRITING

9/19   The beach
- Jumping over waves
- Digging the hole
- Building sand castles
- The Tide

One sunny hot day, we went to the Beach in Maine New hamshre. I loved playing in the sand with my cousins. My cousins were named Thomas, Hannah, Samantha, Makala. My Nana and Papa went, too. My Papa started to dig a little hole. I asked if I could help him with it. He said "I am building a big hole for you, your sister and your cousins. I am defenatly going to need help with the stairs." We worked so hard on the hole all day. Then when my 2 year old cousin, Thomas stepped on the stairs, they colaped! Finaly we got it! We loved playing in the hole. It was about 4 feet deep. The tide came in. We had to move up. When went back down after lunch later that day. It was full of water! It was like a mini swimming pool. Then we came back a few days later and it was gone! The water washed it away! I had fun playing at the beach with my family!.

My mom   9/14
- When she went to Florida
- All About My Mom
- Mommy's cooking

My mom went to Florida. She went for work. She stayed in a hotel room by herself. I wish I could have gone with her. I went with her to her last work confrence. It was in Candy day. I had fun with her. I hope she had fun. She brought back a little pig key chain and a blue pen. I brought my blue pen to school and the red pig chain my sister got. My mom also brought back shoes for me and my little sister. My shoes were were black and Molly's were gray-ich-silver. I wore my new shirt today. It said FLORIDA. I love wearing my new shirt to school. My mom says that I can only wear it once a week. I love my mom! She is AWESOME!

One hot sunny day, we went to the beach in Maine. I love letting the sand run through my toes.

1.

About two hours after we got there, my grandpa started digging a hole. I helped him a little bit. It was so much fun digging the hole. My cousins started to help, too.

2.

BAM!

When we finally got done, the hole was about three or four feet deep. But... when my little cousin steped on the stairs ... **BAM!**

③

The stairs fell down! So, we had to build them all over again. The hole was finaly done. This time the stairs didn't fall down. So, we played in the hole all the rest of the day. We loved playing in the hole.

④

A few days went by and we went back to the beach. We went to the spot that we dug the big hole. The hole was not there! The water had gone in it and the water made the hole disapear! I had so much fun playing at the beach with my cousins and loved digging the big hole!

⑤

FIGURE 8.7 LANGUAGE ANGLED TOWARD SELF-DIRECTED LEARNERS

Say this . . .	Instead of this . . .
It seems to me that you are working on _____. Am I right, or are you working on something else?	Can I tell you the smart thing that you're doing?
I'm thinking that maybe you should work on _____. Does that make sense to you, or would you add to or change anything that I said?	Your job is to work on _____.
I'm noticing _____. *or* I'm thinking _____.	Nice voice. *or* Great details.
I can really picture this part because _____. *or* Do you see how you were the one who did the work here? You thought that you needed help, but in the end you did it yourself.	Good job!

FIGURE 8.8

● Conference Assessment

What was the purpose of this conference? Was it to solve a problem that you'd already established? Was it to engage in a conversation with a student that would extend what he or she was already doing?

Did you notice and name rather than just praise? Is there a way to turn your praise into noticing and naming?

How much child engagement was there? If little or none, what could you have done or said to increase student involvement in the conference?

Was there goal setting at the end? Was the student involved in the goal setting? If not, how could you revise the conference to include the student more?

Did you end with some sort of uncertainty? If not, how could you revise?

© 2013 by Leah Mermelstein from *Self-Directed Writers*. Portsmouth, NH: Heinemann.

Share Sessions That Help Kids Become More Self-Directed

Share sessions are yet another opportunity to teach kids more about writing while at the same time helping them become more self-directed. In my travels, I typically see teachers conduct most of their shares in two different ways. The first type of share I see is the standard author's chair: a student reads his piece and the rest of the class gives the student compliments or suggestions. This type of share is somewhat helpful to the student author, but it's not particularly helpful to the rest of the students. The second type of share is the share that is related to the focus lesson. The student or students who share are the ones who applied what was taught in the focus lesson. The intended goal is that other students will see another example of what was taught, thus furthering their learning. However, many students tune out because they are not the ones sharing.

Following are a few tips to keep in mind as you revise your share sessions so kids learn and become more self-directed. (For a more comprehensive description of share sessions, please refer to my 2007 book *Don't Forget to Share: The Crucial Last Step in the Writing Workshop*.)

Keep All Kids Engaged in the Share Session

To illustrate the importance of shares that keep kids engaged, I return to the collaborative work that Trudy and I did in her classroom. Trudy asked Mason to share how he went from being stuck to unstuck. During this share I brought up the conversation that Mason and I had during the conference. When Mason and I ran out of time, Trudy said she hoped that more kids could share their writing or their experiences from that day. Although I understood her intent, I find that when a share is just giving kids an audience to talk about what they did, the other kids are not engaged. Rather than have lots of kids share either different writing pieces or different ideas, she could have engaged more kids in the share by having a conversation about one thing. I wondered if it would have been more beneficial to use Mason's experience as a way for everyone to talk about what it means to be persistent and if there were times when they either were or were not persistent.

End with Uncertainty

As you can see, uncertainty keeps appearing as a key part of helping kids become more self-directed. Let me give you an example of how uncertainty might play out in a share session. Say a student shares an example of how she tried the technique from the focus lesson. Rather than have just one student share, the teacher might ask all of her students to look at their drafts. They can check to see if the same technique might work in their own pieces of writing. After the student shares, the teacher might say, "I'm not sure this technique will work for all of you, but it is certainly worth a shot. If you don't try it, you won't know if it will work for you. So I want all of you to reread your piece and find a spot to try out the technique. You'll have to decide whether it works for you."

By being uncertain, the teacher leaves the decision of whether the technique works for a particular piece of writing in the hands of each child. They all must try it, but afterward they have to decide whether or not it works. This is an excellent way to scaffold kids in self-regulating their learning. Making their own decisions is bound to make them more excited, engaged, and confident, as well as resourceful. Imagine the difference if the share had ended with more certainty. Imagine if the teacher had said: "I would like all of you to include the technique that was shared in your writing." This type of language makes kids follow directions, rather than make decisions.

End with Goal Setting

End your share sessions by asking kids to consider how they might use what they learned during the share in future writing workshops. You want them to be deliberate and make plans or goals for future work. I watched a teacher conduct a share session where she asked one student to read her writing about getting lost in the woods and not being scared. The other students (rather than just give compliments and suggestions, as in a typical author's chair share) first retold the piece to make sure that they understood what was written and then asked clarifying questions to clear up any confusions they had. One of the kids asked why the student writer wasn't scared and she replied that she wasn't scared because her brother was with her. The teacher then used that question as a jump-start to teach all the kids the importance of considering all the characters in their personal narratives. She said, "So today you all learned how important it can be to introduce the characters early on in your story. This is true for some stories but might not be true for all stories. When it works, it can help your readers better understand your story. Some of you while participating today may have realized that it would be wise to begin tomorrow by rereading your writing to see if it would be helpful to include all of the characters at the start of the story. Speak to the person next to you and let him or her know if this is how you might start tomorrow. You might even want to jot a note on your draft or notebook so you remember this goal tomorrow."

Let Some Share Sessions Provide Kids with Options

As I have said many times in this book, if we want kids to be resourceful during the independent portion of writing workshop, then there must be options for what they can do during writing workshop besides what was taught that day. So far, you've seen how charts and mentor texts give kids other options for what they can do. Share sessions can be another way to give kids options. For example, imagine a teacher, while conferring with a student, helped her add internal thinking to her realistic fiction story. This particular teacher did not teach internal thinking in her focus lesson that day, but it made sense for this student. The teacher then decided to have that student share, not to reinforce the focus lesson but to give the other kids further options on what they could do during the independent portion of writing workshop. The rest of the kids in the class brought their drafts or notebooks with them, but this time they talked about what the teacher did with one student in a conference, rather than what she taught during the focus lesson. During the share session, students tried adding internal thinking in their own pieces of writing to see if it worked. Then the teacher ended the share by saying, "Don't forget that while you are writing during writing workshop you can always help your readers understand your characters more by adding what they were thinking at different points in the story. You can do this whether or not I taught a focus lesson on it."

Figure 8.9 includes sample language you can use in your shares to encourage self-directed writing. You can use the questions in Figure 8.10 to assess how well your shares support self-directed learning.

● Students' Perspectives on Self-Directed Learning

I want to end with a few quotes from some fifth-grade students in Bobbe Pennington's classroom on what they think it means to be self-directed.

- **MIKE:** "You become more independent. You don't have to rely on your parents and teachers to help you."
- **GRACE:** "You don't need to be dependent on others."
- **COLE:** "It's a life lesson. As we grow older, we will be able to do more for ourselves."
- **LISA:** "If you were the last person on Earth, you'd know what to do."
- **KYLE:** "I can think of it in terms of the heart. When you can't think of anything, look inside your heart for answers."

FIGURE 8.9 LANGUAGE ANGLED TOWARD SELF-DIRECTED LEARNERS

Say this . . .	Instead of this . . .
Please bring your draft with you to the share today because after Billy shares what he tried, we'll all reread our drafts to see if it might work for us.	Listen carefully to Billy while he shares his writing.
Reread your draft to see if this strategy might work for you.	Reread your draft and add what Billy shared today into your own draft.
If it does work for you, make a plan in your head (or write one down) so that you know how you'll start tomorrow. *or* Today's share does not connect to what I taught in the focus lesson today. It's something that Samantha tried in her writing that I thought might be helpful to all of you.	That was a great share today.

Inspiring words about an inspiring topic. I hope that while reading this book, you discovered that being self-directed helps your students become more independent so that they don't have to always rely on others. I hope that you discovered that even if your students were the last students on Earth, they would know what to do. And finally, as Kyle said so beautifully, I hope that both you and your students can trust that your heart will lead you to the right answers as you embark on the exciting but messy work of implementing a writing workshop in your classroom.

FIGURE 8.10

● Share Assessment

Did you end your share with some uncertainty as a way to keep the conversation going? If you didn't, is there a way you could revise your share to add uncertainty?

Did you end your share with some sort of planning or goal setting? If you didn't, is there a way you could add planning or goal setting?

Did the share provide kids with options? If it didn't, is there a way you could revise it so kids would have more options?

APPENDIX

● Plan with the End in Mind

Unit Planner for: _____ Teacher: _____

Grade: _____ Length of Study: _____ Month(s) of Study:_____

1. What will the end product look like?

2. How will you celebrate and share learning?

3. Who will be the audience or the readers for your students' writing?

4. What are your goals for this study? (List between two and five.
   These goals will then become part of your assessment systems.)

   a.

   b.

   c.

   d.

   e.

   Don't forget to make a deadline!
   Don't forget to include one goal about self-directed learning.

5. Based on your goals, which books and texts will you use as models and mentors?

● Plan By Studying, Writing, and Reflecting Upon the Experience

Name: _____   Date: _____

1. What did you notice while studying texts?

2. What did you notice while writing your own text?

3. How will this affect the unit of study?

4. Will this affect your goals? If so, how?

The Beginning of the Study: Immersion Notes

Name: _____ Date: _____

1. Studying mentor texts (whole group, partnerships, shares):

2. Write-aloud (possible topics):

Note: If this is a nongenre unit of study, you might want to think about other ways to immerse besides looking at texts.

Name: _____ Date: _____

Possible Focus Lesson Ideas

Drafting:

Revising:

Editing:

Anticipated Problems (e.g., challenges your students face, typical grade-level issues)	Possible Solutions

Name: _____ Date: _____

1. What types of charts might you use (brainstorm charts, language/vocabulary charts, goal charts)?

2. What mentor texts will you use?

3. How can you teach and then display them so that kids will use them independently?

Publishing Notes

Name: _____   Date: _____

1. What will you use as publishing mentors?

2. What type of chart will support publishing?

3. How will you encourage students to be self-directed?

Following is an example based on goals created by a group of upper-grade teachers.

	4	3	2	1
Oral rehearsal	I was able to defend my position to a partner including multiple pieces of evidence as well as a counterargument.	I was able to defend my position to a partner including multiples pieces of evidence.	I was able to defend my position to a partner including limited evidence.	I was unable to defend my position to a partner.
Arguments	I built my argument in multiple ways (personal story, research, survey, etc.) and was able to figure out which ways were best for my writing piece.	I built my argument in multiple ways.	I built my argument in a few ways.	I was unable to build my argument.
Writer's Notebook	I tried out many different planning strategies in my notebook and have a clear understanding of how each strategy improved my draft.	I tried out many different planning strategies and have some understanding about how those strategies improved my draft.	I tried out a few planning strategies in my notebook and have some understanding of how these improved my draft.	I did not try out any strategies in my notebook.
Using class resources	I always used classroom resources to help me complete classroom work as well as try out additional things independently.	I usually used classroom resources to help me complete classroom work as well as try out additional things independently.	I sometimes used classroom resources to fulfill classroom work.	I never used classroom resources to fulfill classroom work.

- At the end of this unit, students will be able to orally rehearse their evidence for their argument with a partner.
- At the end of this unit, students will understand multiple ways to build their argument (personal example, research, survey, etc.).
- At the end of this unit, students will understand how to use their writer's notebooks to plan their persuasive essays.
- At the end of this unit, students will understand how to use classroom resources independently to solve problems and get things accomplished.

The next assessment is an example based on goals created by a group of third-grade teachers.

	4	3	2	1
Organization	My entire draft is organized into categories that are easy to understand.	Most of my draft is organized into categories that are fairly easy to understand.	Some of my draft is organized into categories.	My draft is not organized into catego-ries and is difficult to understand.
Facts that define	I included many facts that define, and the definitions are specific and clear.	I included many facts that define, and the defini-tions are usually specific and clear.	I included some facts that define, and the defini-tions are vague and unclear.	I did not include facts that define.
Facts that describe	I included many descriptive facts and composed these facts using a lot of sensory language.	I included some descriptive facts and composed these facts using some sensory language.	I included some descriptive facts and composed these facts using limited sensory language.	I did not include descriptive facts.
Literary language	I used a lot of literary language in my draft and ensured that I used it in appropriate ways.	I used some literary language in my draft and ensured that I used it in appro-priate ways.	I used limited literacy lan-guage and I am unsure if I used it in appropriate ways.	I did not include literary language.

The original goals of this unit:

- At the end of this unit, kids will understand how to organize their information into categories.
- At the end of this unit, kids will understand how to write facts that define.
- At the end of this unit, kids will understand how to write facts that describe.
- At the end of this unit, kids will understand how to include informational book language in their writing (e.g., *some, all, many, for example, another*).

Name: _____ Date: _____

1. What went well? Why did it go well?

2. What was difficult? Why might it have been difficult?
   What can you do next time to change this?

WORKS CITED

Anderson, Carl. 2000. *How's It Going? A Practical Guide to Conferring with Student Writers.* Portsmouth, NH: Heinemann.

———. 2005. *Assessing Writers.* Portsmouth, NH: Heinemann.

———. 2009. *Strategic Writing Conferences: Smart Conversations That Move Young Writers Forward, Grades 3–6.* Portsmouth, NH: Heinemann.

Brush, Thomas A., and John W. Saye. 2002. "A Summary of Research Exploring Hard and Soft Scaffolding for Teachers and Students Using a Multimedia Supported Learning Environment." *Journal of Interactive Online Learning* 1 (2): 1–12.

Calkins, Lucy. 2003. *The Nuts and Bolts of Teaching Writing.* Units of Study for Primary Writing: A Yearlong Curriculum (K–2). Portsmouth, NH: FirstHand.

Calkins, Lucy, and Colleagues from the Teachers College Reading and Writing Project. 2003. *Units of Study for Primary Writing: A Yearlong Curriculum (K–2).* Portsmouth, NH: FirstHand.

———. 2006. *Units of Study for Teaching Writing, Grades 3–5.* Portsmouth, NH: FirstHand.

Early Head Start National Resources Center at Zero to Three. 1992. *The Foundations for School Readiness: Fostering Developmental Competence in the Earliest Years.* Technical Assistance Paper No. 6. Washington, DC: US Dept. of Health and Human Services.

Fletcher, Ralph. 1993. *What a Writer Needs.* Portsmouth, NH: Heinemann.

Fountas, Irene, and Gay Su Pinnell. 1996. *Guided Reading: Good First Teaching for All Children.* Portsmouth, NH: Heinemann.

Glover, Matt, and Mary Alice Berry. 2012. *Projecting Possibilities for Writers: The How, What and Why of Designing Units of Study, K–5.* Portsmouth, NH: Heinemann.

Guglielmino, Lucy M. 1978. "Development of the Self-Directed Learning Readiness Scale." Abstract. Doctoral diss., University of Georgia, 1977. *Dissertation Abstracts International* 38: 6467A.

Johnston, Peter. 2012. *Opening Minds: Using Language to Change Lives.* Portland, ME: Stenhouse Publishers.

Katz, Lilian G., and Sylvia C. Chard. 1989. *Engaging Children's Minds: The Project Approach.* Norwood, NJ: Ablex.

Laminack, Lester. 2009. Keynote Speech. Literacy for All Conference, Providence, RI, November 15–17.

Martinelli, Marjorie, and Kristine Mraz. 2012. *Smarter Charts, K–2: Optimizing an Instructional Staple to Create Independent Readers and Writers*. Portsmouth, NH: Heinemann.

Mermelstein, Leah. 2007. *Don't Forget to Share: The Crucial Last Step in the Writing Workshop*. Portsmouth, NH: Heinemann.

Nor, Mariani, and Y. Saeednia. 2009. "Exploring Self-Directed Learning among Children." *International Journal of Human and Social Sciences* 4 (9): 658–63.

Oczkus, Lori. 2007. *Guided Writing: Practical Lessons, Powerful Results*. Portsmouth, NH: Heinemann.

Rock, David. 2006. *Quiet Leadership: Help People Think Better—Don't Tell Them What to Do: Six Steps to Transforming Performance at Work*. New York: Collins.

Routman, Regie. 2005. *Writing Essentials: Raising Expectations and Results While Simplifying Teaching*. Portsmouth, NH: Heinemann.

Sawyer, R. Keith. 2006. *The Cambridge Handbook of the Learning Sciences*. New York: Cambridge University Press.

Taberski, Sharon. 2011. *Comprehension from the Ground Up: Simplified, Sensible Instruction for the K–3 Reading Workshop*. Portsmouth, NH: Heinemann.

Wiggins, Grant, and Jay McTighe. 2005. *Understanding by Design*. Alexandria, VA: Association for Supervision and Curriculum Development.

Zimmerman, B. J. 2000. "Attaining Self-Regulation: A Social Cognitive Perspective." In *Handbook of Self-Regulation*, ed. Monique Boekaerts, Paul R. Pintrich, and Moshe Zeidner, 13–39. San Diego: Academic Press.